Yachts on Canvas

Artists' Images of Yachts from the Seventeenth Century to the Present Day

To Stefania, Joshua and Luke

Yachts on Canvas

Artists' Images of
Yachts from the
Seventeenth Century
to the Present Day

JAMES TAYLOR

KNICKERBOCKER
PRESS

Frontispiece

◆

ROYAL FORTH YACHT REGATTA, GRANTON, 25 JULY 1859
(Detail)

John Watson McLea (active 1832–1861)
(oil on canvas, 82.5 x 117cm, dated 1859)
The Royal Forth Yacht Club.

The regatta was organised by the Royal Eastern Yacht Club, which was established in 1835 and incorporated into the Royal Forth Yacht Club in 1969. The regatta commodore was Lord John Scott, vice-commodore of the yacht club. His yacht, *The Flower of Yarrow*, is shown here dressed overall and flying the burgee and ensign of the Royal Eastern Yacht Club.

McLea is a little-known Scottish marine, landscape and portrait painter who deserves greater recognition. He worked in Leith, a suburb of Edinburgh and exhibited at the Royal Scottish Academy.

Published by Knickerbocker Press,
276 Fifth Avenue,
New York, NY 10001

This edition © 1998

ISBN 1-57715-050-3

Text © James Taylor, 1998

Volume © Conway Maritime Press, 1998

First published in Great Britain in 1998 by
Conway Maritime Press

Designed by Peter Champion

Origination by Bright Arts Ltd, Hong Kong
Printed and bound by Imago Ltd, Singapore

Acknowledgements

Of the many people who have contributed their enthusiasm, knowledge and experience to this publication, I would like to single out the following for special mention. The first is Glen S Foster, whose insight into the remarkable yachting scenes of J E Buttersworth, and many other American and European maritime artists, professional yachting experience and advice at all levels have been invaluable. It would be no exaggeration to say that without his assistance this book would not have been possible. John Egan, Jan-Willem Broekhuysen, Philip Banks, Patrick McHugh and Jacqui English of A T Kearney, London, had the imagination to host a yachting exhibition at the company's headquarters. *Yachts on Canvas* was the first yachting exhibition to be held in a corporate environment. The exercise opened my eyes to the varied categories of yachting art and presented the creative challenge of how they might be expressed in an exhibition format.

The following individuals and organisations have all assisted magnanimously in this project: Dr Alicia St Leger; Commander David Joel, Curator, the Royal Yacht Squadron; Captain A R Ward, Archivist, the Royal Thames Yacht Club; Dermot Burns, Archivist, the Royal Cork Yacht Club; Gerald Glancy, Archivist, the Royal Forth Yacht Club; Robert McKay and Joe Jackson, Librarian, the New York Yacht Club; the artists: Don Demers, William Davis, Christopher Blossom, Richard Loud, John Mecray, A D Blake, David Cobb, John Stobart, Roy Cross, David Brackman, Michael Vaughan, Geoff Hunt, Mark Myers, Gerald Savine, J Steven Dews, Martyn Mackrill and Rowena Wright; the art galleries, museums, auction houses and dealers: the Royal Collection; Tina Chambers and Chris Gray, National Maritime Museum, Greenwich; Remmelt Daalder, Nederlands Scheepvaartmuseum, Amsterdam; Annie Madet, Musée de la Marine; Philip Budlong, Mystic Seaport Gallery; Richard Newbury, Sotheby's; Joe Vallejo and Marcus de Chevrieux, Vallejo Maritime Gallery; Allan Granby, Hyland Granby Antiques; Susan Gregory, the Gregory Gallery; Tom Geary, Geary Gallery; The Old Print Shop; David Green and Susan Morris, Richard Green Galleries; Oliver Swann, Tryon & Swann Gallery; Roger and Jill Hadlee, Royal Exchange Gallery; Kenneth Kendall; Colin Denny, Laurence Langford, Langfords Marine Antiques; Juliet Johnson and Tony Nevill, Frost & Reed; Charles Omell and Marian Earnest, N R Omell Gallery and Stephen Bartley, Bartley Drey Gallery. Anthony J Peluso Jr, Bob McKenna, Nautical World, Dr James Dickie, A D F Dalton, Sandra M Heaphy, Mrs F Wagner, Nancy Attwood and Aldo Caterino have all given invaluable help. Also John Lee, Nicki Marshall, Sylvia Monkhouse, Peter Champion and the team at Conway Maritime Press, who brought the project to fruition.

Ranulf Rayner has granted permission to reproduce the image of *Britannia* by Tim Thompson. This is one of a series of twenty-six prints entitled 'The Paintings of the America's Cup and The Great Yachts' published by Ashcombe Fine Arts, Dawlish, Devon, England. National Maritime Museum prints are available from Photographic Services, National Maritime Museum, Romney Road, Greenwich, SE10 9NF.

Contents

Introduction

MENTION THE WORD 'YACHT' AND MOST PEOPLE WILL CONJURE UP IMAGES OF SLEEK OCEAN RACERS BATTLING AGAINST THE ELEMENTS ON THE HIGH SEAS. IN FACT, THE TERM COVERS A SURPRISINGLY WIDE RANGE OF VESSELS OF VARYING SIZES, RIGS AND MEANS OF PROPULSION.

In his classic work *Yachts and Yachting in Contemporary Art*, published in 1925, the late B Heckstall-Smith, a leading authority on yachting, defined the yacht as a 'craft of considerable dimensions, not plying for hire, and devoted to pleasure'. He believed that the earliest literary reference to such a craft was Plutarch's account of the journey that Cleopatra made across the Mediterranean to visit Anthony. According to Plutarch, writing in the first century AD, Cleopatra had sailed 'in a vessel, the stern whereof was gold, the sails of purple silk, and the oars of silver, which gently kept time to the sound of music'.

Yachting as we know it today originated in the seventeenth century in the Netherlands, where yachts were used to transport important officials, and occasionally to race. This new sport soon spread to England, where in 1661 Charles II raced his yacht *Katherine* against his brother James, Duke of York. The golden age of yachting really began in the early nineteenth century, when wealthy yacht owners in Britain and the United States formed clubs and organised races. While some of these races have lasted to this day, the yachts themselves have developed considerably over the years. Steam, gas turbines, and diesel and petrol engines, as well as highly sophisticated rigs, have all been used to make yachts faster.

Even in his own day, Heckstall-Smith's definition of the vessel was too restrictive. The distinction between business and pleasure in relation to yachts, especially royal yachts, has always been a difficult one to make. For instance, the presence of the British royal yacht *Britannia* in foreign ports and the on-board hospitality of the royal family, has no doubt played a major part in securing lucrative business for Britain. Indeed, one of the arguments advanced to support the construction of a new royal yacht is that she would continue this vital role. Yachting has, in fact, long been associated with the promotion of companies and products, notably Lipton's tea. Recently, leisure and telecommunications, among many other goods and services, have received increased attention by sponsoring yachting events.

Previous pages

◆

COLUMBIA VERSUS SHAMROCK I, 1899

(Detail)

John Mecray (b.1937)
(oil on canvas, 61 x 112cm, dated 1994)
Courtesy of the artist.

This work shows Sir Thomas Lipton's first attempt to challenge for the America's Cup with *Shamrock I*, designed by William Fife, Jr. The green gaff-rigged sloop measured 129ft overall, 90ft on the water with a 25ft beam. The Nathaniel Herreshoff-designed *Columbia* beat *Shamrock I*, the tenth successive win for the New York Yacht Club. It was the first of five unsuccessful challenges by Lipton with yachts of the same name. His final attempt was in 1930, when *Enterprise* defeated *Shamrock V*.

John Mecray is a leading American maritime artist with a passion for painting yachts. He studied illustration and painting at the Philadelphia College of Art. He played the key part in the foundation of the Museum of Yachting in Newport, Rhode Island, and the museum's annual Classic Yacht Regatta. He has also been actively involved in the restoration of *Shamrock V*. Mecray creates images of historic and contemporary yachts in a cool, classical style which has stimulated enthusiasm in people who would not normally be interested in yachting subjects, or for that matter maritime painting.

Although yachts still convey heads of state, officials and the well-to-do, yachting is no longer solely the prerogative of the rich and famous. As the celebrated yachtsman Sir Robin Knox-Johnston has noted, 'Huge yachts with their large paid crews are only the most glamorous part of the story.' Since the end of the nineteenth century many less-wealthy people have raced smaller boats requiring only a one-man or limited crew; and in recent years, windsurfing has become one of the most popular forms of yachting and one of the most accessible of all water sports, enjoyed by thousands around the world.

Today the range of the sport is enormous. It encompasses competitive day-sailing in large and small boats, and long-distance sailing in yachts managed single-handedly or by crews of up to twenty or more. It also covers the activities of the vast majority of people who just enjoy cruising with family and friends.

Artists have been fascinated by yachts for almost four hundred years. While some have recorded the ceremonial pomp of royal fleet reviews and other state yachting occasions, others have tried to capture the thrills and dangers of ocean racing, circumnavigations and voyages of discovery.

Perhaps the best-known category of yachting art is the yacht portrait, that is a picture which shows a vessel in full sail or battling against treacherous conditions. Such works concentrate primarily on the nautical detail of the yacht itself, and the background sea or landscape features are of less importance.

Some household names, such as J M W Turner and Claude Monet, had first-hand experience of yachting, and painted racing and regatta scenes in their well-known styles. However, these painters are beyond the scope of this publication. The focus of *Yachts on Canvas* is on the many, less-familiar

artists, working mainly in Europe, especially in Britain, and North America, who had or have an intimate knowledge of their subject as well as the skills required to translate this into prints, drawings, watercolours and oil paintings.

Among those featured here are the prominent seventeenth-century marine artists Willem van de Velde the Elder (1611–1693) and his son, also called Willem (1633–1707), who painted some of the earliest images of Dutch and English yachts. Also discussed are Tomaso, or Tommaso, de Simone (active 1850–1900) and Antonio de Simone (active 1860–1920),

A States Yacht in a Fresh Breeze

Willem van de Velde the Younger (1633–1707)
(oil on canvas, 75 x 108cm, dated 1673)
National Maritime Museum, Greenwich.

The Steam Yacht *Narada*, off Naples

Antonio de Simone (active 1860–1920)
(gouache on paper, 42 x 64.5cm, dated 1898)
Vallejo Maritime Gallery.

In the seventeenth century, the Dutch Republic was made up of seven provinces, known as *staten*, or states, each of which had its own yachts for official use. Together these states formed the States General, to which the yacht in the right foreground probably belonged. Notice the elaborate carving and gilding on its stern. Yachts conveyed wealth and status, and fortunes were lavished on them. Artists such as the van de Veldes were sometimes commissioned to decorate the vessels. In addition, they also produced oil paintings to adorn the cabin interiors.

William van de Velde the Younger adopts the Dutch artistic conventions of a low viewpoint and dominant sky here. The rendering of wind against the sails and flags, and the movement of the sea and vessels, is handled with consummate skill.

A particularly fine example by Antonio de Simone of the steam yacht *Narada*. Built by Ramage and Ferguson in 1889, the yacht was originally named *Semiramis*. She was a screw brigantine weighing 491 gross tons. Her designer, A H Brown, was a ship's master who turned to yacht design. Later purchased by Henry Walters, founder of the Walters Art Gallery in Baltimore, she became one of the best-known yachts in Europe during her owner's trips to acquire art works.

Little is known about the de Simones, but they were probably father and son. Neapolitan yacht portraits, usually painted in gouache, an opaque form of watercolour, are atmospheric and of great charm, although they invariably lack precise nautical detail. Many are unsigned, and are attributed simply as 'Neapolitan School'.

the most famous of the numerous artists working in nineteenth-century Naples who painted yacht portraits for wealthy owners cruising in the Mediterranean. They produced large numbers of these pictures, usually with Mount Vesuvius as a dramatic backdrop, as souvenirs for yacht owners to hang on board their vessels or in their homes back on dry land. Scenes of holidays afloat, whether they be cruises aboard large ocean-going yachts or people just simply messing about in small sailing-boats, continue to attract the attention of artists today.

The nineteenth-century painters James Edward Buttersworth (1817–1894) and Nicholas Matthews Condy (1818–1851) rank as two of the finest of all yachting artists. In many instances they were eye-witness recorders of the celebrated regattas of the nineteenth century. These historic events remain by far the most popular subject of yachting art today. Other favourites include the great races, especially those of the America's Cup and the 1920s and 1930s, the era of the short-lived big J-class yachts, memorable for their graceful lines and vast areas of sail.

HIGH WATER, TENBY

Arthur James Weatherall Burgess (1879–1957)
(oil on canvas, 46 x 61cm, circa 1950)
Courtesy of Stephen Bartley.

A peaceful composition of various yachts, dinghies and tenders. Sir Thomas Lipton's steam yacht *Erin* can be seen in the distance, identifiable by the yellow funnel. Lipton used *Erin* for cruising and to follow the progress of his challenges for the America's Cup.

Originally from Bombola, New South Wales, Burgess studied in Sydney and also in St Ives in Cornwall, before settling in London. He is better known as an illustrator and official war artist, working during the Second World War. He painted a wide range of maritime subjects, including yachts usually by a quayside or in harbour. He also painted landscape subjects, including ski resorts.

THE SCHOONER YACHT *AMERICA*

Nineteenth-Century American Primitive School
(oil on canvas, 76 x 91.5cm, circa 1855)
New York Yacht Club.

On 22 August 1851, in a race round the Isle of Wight, the schooner yacht *America* finished first of sixteen yachts to win the Hundred-Guinea Cup presented by the Royal Yacht Squadron. The cup was made by the London jewellers R & G Garrard and took its name from its original price. It was renamed the America's Cup, after the winning schooner, and has yet to be won by a British yacht club.

America is portrayed here by an unknown American artist. Despite the painter's limited artistic skill this portrait possesses considerable charm. Note the oversized flags and figures aboard. Launched in 1851, the yacht survived until 1942, when, laid up in Annapolis, Maryland, she was destroyed in a snowstorm.

Of the many modern artists tackling historical yachting subjects such as these, Roy Cross (b.1924) and J Steven Dews (b.1949) rate highly among the leading British practitioners, while Frank Wagner (1931–1996), and John Mecray (b.1937) are two of the best-known American artists. Wagner was a keen sailor and was part-owner of *American Eagle*, which put the famous American yacht *Constellation* through her paces and prepared her for a successful defence of the America's Cup in 1964 against *Sovereign*, the Royal Thames Yacht Club's challenger.

Many other marine painters, too, have also been enthusiastic yachtsmen, and some, including the American artist Archibald Cary Smith (1837–1911), excelled as yacht designers as well. Others made a living turning out highly finished colour prints for yacht designers and owners, yachtsmen and maritime enthusiasts. A few fortunate individuals became honorary artists to yachting clubs, a post which usually ensured a regular flow of commissions from club members. Others, for example the Australian artist Arthur James Weatherall Burgess (1879–1957), William

SHAMROCK III AND *RELIANCE*, AMERICA'S CUP RACING OFF SANDY HOOK, 1903

Frank Wagner (1931–1996)
(gouache on board, 62 x 50cm, dated 1995)
Courtesy of Mrs Frank Wagner.

The 1903 race for the America's Cup off Sandy Hook, New Jersey, is viewed here from the foredeck of a large vintage steam yacht crowded with guests. Both racing boats are off to a fair start up the windward leg of the course. In the event, Sir Thomas Lipton's challenge in *Shamrock III* was a disappointment since the *Reliance*, designed by Herreshoff, proved unbeatable.

Wagner's ability to create striking compositions, his interest in close-up detail and the prominence he gives to figures in his pictures, reveal his grounding in the art of commercial illustration. It is certainly the key to the American artist's popularity with collectors. Wagner was born on Long Island, New York. After studying at the Pennsylvania Academy of Fine Arts, Philadelphia, and at the Pratt Institute, New York, he was awarded a European Fellowship grant at the Rijksmuseum School in Amsterdam. In the last years of his life, Wagner lived and worked on the east coast of England.

Lionel Wyllie (1851–1931), and Montague Dawson (1895–1973), worked as roving 'visual journalists' providing representations of yachting scenes for illustrated weekly newspapers. Peter MacDonagh Wood (1914–1982) also worked as an illustrator for various yachting magazines until the demand for artists' illustrational work largely dried up in the 1930s.

In the late twentieth century, both yachting art and yachting itself have undergone remarkable transformations. The development of photography, film and video, which can more easily capture the action of yacht racing, has seen a reduction in commissions for the more traditional yacht portraits and race scenes; and improved designs and technology now enable yachts to sail faster for longer. Some artists, among them Michael Vaughan and John Mecray, have responded to these changes by turning their attention towards producing striking images of unusual or little-recorded aspects of yacht racing. Others, such as Rowena Wright, one of the few successful woman marine artists, prefer to capture the envigorating but demanding experiences of the crew as they speed across the waves.

THE YACHT *GIPSY MOTH IV* RUNNING BEFORE A QUARTERING SEA

Peter MacDonagh Wood (1914–1982)
(oil on canvas, 61 x 91.5cm, circa 1967)
National Maritime Museum, Greenwich.

Francis Chichester (1901–1972) was the first man to sail single-handedly around the world. Setting off from Plymouth on 27 August 1966, he completed the one-stop voyage in 226 days, at the time a record circumnavigation. His vessel, *Gipsy Moth IV*, was a 54ft ketch designed by the British designers Illingworth and Primrose to a brief that it should be capable of sailing to Sydney in a hundred days. Upon his return, Chichester was knighted by Queen Elizabeth II at the Royal Naval College, Greenwich, with the sword that Queen Elizabeth I had used in 1581 to knight Sir Francis Drake after his circumnavigation in the *Golden Hind*.

Peter MacDonagh Wood was a keen yachtsman and executed many illustrations of yachting subjects. He studied art in Southend, Hornsey and at the Slade in London. He also advised the British film industry on maritime matters.

For many years, yachting art has rarely been considered worthy of serious study. Consequently, in most cases very little, or next to nothing, was known about the artists featured in *Yachts on Canvas*. Much of the information presented here is new material, only recently gleaned from a wide variety of primary and secondary sources. For this reason the book is the most comprehensive and up-to-date work on the subject.

Fine examples from the art collections of the Royal Cork Yacht Club, the Royal Thames Yacht Club, the Royal Yacht Squadron at Cowes and the New York Yacht Club, as well as from maritime museums, auction houses, dealers and private collections, have been brought together, many for the first time, in *Yachts on Canvas*. These images will be of interest not only to yachting historians, designers and enthusiasts, recording as they do the development of the vessels and the sport over the centuries, but also to collectors, art historians, dealers, and anyone who loves marine art. It is hoped that the book will play a part, albeit a small one, in the general reassessment of this much neglected genre.

Left

◆

THE YACHT *SEA CLOUD*

Montague Dawson (1895–1973)
(oil on canvas, 38 x 46.5cm, circa 1960)
Vallejo Maritime Gallery. Reproduced by
permission of the executors of the estate of
Montague Dawson.

Square-rigged and barque-rigged sailing vessels have also been used as yachts. The 316ft *Sea Cloud* (ex-*Hussar*) was built by the German Krupp shipyard in 1931. She has had a colourful history. She was owned by the American heiress Marjorie Post, and later sold to the Dominican dictator, Rafael Trujillo. In the 1950s, she could be seen sailing the southern Californian coast, and was a popular attraction for the Hollywood film set. Prior to the Second World War, *Sea Cloud* was used by Marjorie Post's second husband, US Ambassador Joseph E Davies, for diplomatic entertaining.

Montague Dawson has been described as the 'king of the clipper-ship artists'. Indeed this British-born artist did specialise in graceful and stately portraits of merchantmen set in magnificent seas of swirling colour. His yachting paintings are less well known but are highly accomplished and are certainly worthy of more attention.

MAXI-CLASS YACHTS RACING OFF SARDINIA, 1995

Michael Vaughan (b.1940)
(oil on canvas, 68.5 x 94cm, dated 1995)
Courtesy of the artist.

This dramatic, close-up composition, which carefully describes the on-board equipment of the yachts, is typical of Vaughan's work. In many of his pictures he makes a feature of the state-of-the-art technology that pushes the vessels to ever greater levels of performance. Here, traditional wood and canvas have given way to lighter and stronger high-tech materials. The aerodynamic shapes of the yachts' hulls provide striking contrasts.

Vaughan is one of the most exciting British marine painters working today. He has moved away from conventional methods of portraying yachts on canvas to explore new avenues of expression, drawing inspiration from photography, film, video and computer graphics in his attempts to capture the vigour, excitement, speed and grace of ocean racing.

CHAPTER I

The Early Years of Yachting

YACHTING HAS ITS ORIGINS IN THE SHELTERED WATERS OF THE NETHERLANDS. IN FACT, THE WORD 'YACHT' IS DERIVED FROM THE DUTCH *JACHT*, WHICH ITSELF COMES FROM THE VERB 'TO HURRY' OR 'TO HUNT'. ORIGINALLY, THE WORD DESCRIBED ANY FAST SAILING SHIP OR BOAT.

In the mid-seventeenth century, such boats were mainly used for official business to transport the government personnel and dignitaries of the seven provinces forming the Dutch Republic. These provinces were known as *staten*, or states, and their yachts were called States yachts. Various other government bodies, such as the States General – the collective assembly of the seven provinces – and the Admiralty boards, also had their own States yachts.

At the time, the Dutch Republic was a major maritime power, and the most prosperous country in Europe. In towns and cities such as Amsterdam and Delft large numbers of successful merchants were busy earning massive fortunes. Many of these spent their money on impressive town and country houses or on expensive yachts. The country's prosperity was largely based on the worldwide trading activities of the Dutch East India Company. The company, too, owned yachts, which, confusingly, were also called States yachts. It used them for carrying dispatches and officials, as well as for leisure. It also frequently organised informal yacht races.

Increased trade was reflected in a lively art market. This was the golden age of Dutch painting, the era of Rembrandt, Hals and Vermeer. State officials, city guilds, trading companies and individual merchants, all of whom were proud of their own successes, commissioned artists to commemorate their achievements on canvas. Some had their portraits painted showing them wearing their finest clothes. Some preferred to have themselves painted with their families in domestic or social settings. Others commissioned exquisite still lifes depicting luxury goods, such as gold and silver plates and goblets, or opulent displays of flowers and food. A familiar feature of Dutch painting from this period is its accurate detail, perhaps reflecting patrons' concerns with all things material. Fine silks and lace, intricate interior decorations, and rotten, decaying apples are all rendered with such skilful precision that they seem almost real.

Maritime merchants were also eager to record their achievements on canvas, and many commissioned the leading artists of the day to paint portraits of their cargo ships and private vessels. Until this time oil paintings of marine subjects were relatively rare, and artists had to look elsewhere for models which they could follow. Many took their inspiration from cartography, adopting the convention of a high viewpoint to show a scene from above, rather like a map or plan of the action. This helped early yachting artists make visual sense of a sometimes complex subject. Some early yachting art also included a key to assist the viewer.

One of the earliest recorded images in oils of yachts racing was painted in the 1630s by the Antwerp artist Andries van Eertvelt (*see pages 14–15*). The work was probably commissioned by the owner of the victorious boat. Eertvelt painted in a theatrical, non-naturalistic style known as Flemish mannerism. He was less concerned with painting realistically, and used artificial colours and fanciful compositions. At first glance, it is difficult to make out exactly what is happening in this vivid and dramatic picture. Several boats have become victims of the violent storm, and some terrified sailors have raised their arms in fear. Notice the seamen's colourful apparel, and the orange and blue hair of the sailors,

Previous pages

◆

DUTCH WORKING BOATS AND YACHTS RACING
(Detail)

Andries van Eertvelt (1590–1652)
(oil on canvas, 123 x 201.5cm, circa 1630)
National Maritime Museum, Greenwich.

It appears as if the yacht, seen to the immediate left of the illuminated sail, has rounded the mark first and is in the lead. The elaborate carving on the stern, and the figure on board with an orange feather in his hat, indicate that it is likely to be a Dutch royal yacht. The flag on the working boat to the far left is that of the City of Amsterdam.

Originally from Antwerp in modern-day Belgium, Eertvelt worked mainly in Holland. He was almost certainly a pupil of Hendrik Cornelisz Vroom (1566–1640), now considered the founding father of marine painting. Eertvelt's early works are fine examples of the non-naturalistic Flemish mannerist style. His dark, green seas are punctuated with brilliant highlights of colour. His subjects included general shipping scenes, stormy scenes and shipwrecks. He often used the convention of a high viewpoint, popular with early marine painters, indicating his familiarity with cartography.

which certainly derived from the painter's imagination. Another of the Flemish mannerists was Adam Willaerts (1577–1664), who painted yachting scenes in his own individual and distinctive style (*see page 19*).

Responding to changing tastes, artists of the following generations rejected Flemish mannerism and produced far more realistic works. Among them are Willem van de Velde the Elder (1611–1693), and his son, Willem the Younger (1633–1707), now widely acknowledged as two of the finest of all marine artists. Although van de Velde the Elder occasionally painted in oils, his work mainly consists of drawings. He was one of the earliest practitioners of an artistic technique known as *penschildering*, or pen-painting, often called *grisaille*. In this, quill pens are used to create sharp lines on panels or canvas which are sometimes highlighted with grey wash. Using this technique, artists could create far more detailed works than they could with oils, and pen-paintings became the nautical equivalent of the still lifes. Although they took much longer to complete than oil paintings, pen-painted works, which in many ways resembled engravings, were much admired by naval officers, mariners, merchants and yacht owners who demanded above all accuracy and exacting detail.

Van de Velde the Elder could provide such accurate nautical detail because he had practical experience of the subject. Before becoming an artist, he had had a brief career at sea. He may also have owned a number of yachts that he used for both work and pleasure. He often used a small vessel as a floating studio, going out on the water, with a sketch pad on his knee, to make on-the-spot drawings, which either he or his son would work up into a painting back on dry land. The time involved in oil painting, and the size of the canvases, made it impossible to work on board yachts. Some artists observed from ashore, instead, or based their work on eye-witness accounts.

Willem the Younger surpassed his father as an oil painter. His popularity lies in his ability to create accurate, animated and harmonious compositions, and in his expert handling of naturalistic and atmospheric effects. That he could produce such faithful accounts of yachting was because, like his father, he had first-hand knowledge of the practice. He often sketched yachts in action, and he may also have been a yachtsman. The inscription on one of his studies reads 'To be noted: a ship or small vessel in pitching nearly always throws up spray, as shown here'. A series of ten sketch plans now held in the National Maritime Museum, Greenwich, (*see page 22*) reveal that van de Velde the Younger was probably also designing a yacht for himself.

During the English Civil War, King Charles II lived in exile in the Dutch Republic. He was entranced by the many types of yachts sailing on the country's inland waterways and around its coast. In addition to the States yachts there were *spiegeljacht*, or tafferel yachts, *paviljoenjacht* – the *paviljoen* being a raised cabin in the stern – and even *spiegelpaviljoenjacht*. Charles soon became a yachting enthusiast, and in 1660 the Dutch East India Company presented him with a yacht, the *Mary*. Although the vessel was actually a miniature warship, she was designed for private cruising. The *Mary* conveyed Charles II on part of his journey home to England the following year. The Dutch also presented the king with the *Bezan* (*see page 20*), an example of one of the most common Dutch yachts, the *bezaanjacht*.

After Charles II's restoration to the English throne in 1661, the diarist John Evelyn noted on 1 October: 'I sail'd this morning with his Majesty in one of his yachts (or pleasure boats), vessells not known among us 'til the Dutch E[ast] India Company presented that curious piece to the King, being very excellent sailing vessells.' Samuel Pepys also thought it worthy to write about the *Mary* 'from whence came the improvements of our present yachts; for until that time we had not heard such a name in England.'

Charles II had enjoyed yacht racing during his exile, and upon his return to England he introduced the sport to his own country. In 1661, he raced against his brother, the Duke of York (later King James II), on the Thames for a wager of £100. According to John Evelyn who accompanied the king in the *Katherine* during the race, 'The King lost in the going, the wind being contrary, but saved stakes in returning.' From this account, it would appear that the first recorded race in England ended in a draw.

During the Restoration period, yacht design moved away from the Dutch models to the beautiful English smack-rigged yachts. Their main role was to carry dispatches or courtiers and their guests around the British coast, and to and from the Continent. Charles II also used them for racing. In 1661, the king converted the *Surprise*, the coasting collier in which he had escaped from England ten years earlier, to a smack-rigged yacht and renamed her *Royal Escape*. She was kept moored in the Thames opposite Whitehall Palace 'as a reminder to himself and his subjects.'

Willem van de Velde the Younger painted the *Royal Escape* in around 1675 (*see page 21*). He and his father had arrived in England in 1672 or 1673 after Charles II had made an open invitation to European artists to settle in England. They were short of work after the recent French invasion of the Dutch Republic had disrupted trade and decimated the art market.

After their arrival in England, the van de Veldes both painted a number of royal yachts. Among Willem van de Velde the Elder's paintings of this period is *Calm: the English Yacht* Portsmouth of 1675 (*see pages 24–5*). The yacht had been named the previous year by Charles II after his mistress, the Duchess of Portsmouth. He had earlier named a yacht *Cleveland*, after another mistress, Barbara Villiers, Duchess of Cleveland. The *Cleveland* is traditionally identified as the foreground vessel in van de Velde the Younger's *English Royal Yachts at Sea* of 1689 (*see page 26*).

Charles II was quick to appreciate the talents of the van de Veldes and was anxious to retain their services. He instructed the Treasurer of the Navy to pay the 'salary of One hundred pounds per annum unto William Vandeveld the elder for taking and making of Draughts [drawings] of Sea Fights, and the like Salary of One Hundred pounds per annum unto William Vandeveld the younger for putting the said draughts into Colours [oil paintings] for Our particular use'. At the time, this was a great deal of money.

The king also provided the van de Veldes with studio space in the Queen's House in Greenwich, now part of the National Maritime Museum. The royal villa was designed by Inigo Jones and completed for Henrietta Maria, consort of King Charles I, in around 1638. A number of assistants were lured to help the van de Veldes in their studio, which explains the existence of a large body of their work. The father-and-son team were catering for a wide circle of patrons, which extended far beyond the confines of England and included private collectors in Holland, Denmark, and Italy. Not all of the van de Veldes' pictures were considered successful, however. They had a tendency of regularly repeating compositions, making their work seem at times formulaic and dull. Even so, their presence stimulated a general interest in England in marine painting and yachting subjects, and their influence on English yachting art was felt well into the eighteenth century.

Several Dutch artists worked in, or were associated with, the van de Velde studio in Greenwich, including Johan van der Hagen (1645–*c*.1720),

Adriaen van Diest (1655–1704), Cornelis van de Velde (1675–1729) and L d Man (active 1707–1725). All of them copied and adapted the van de Veldes' work with varying degrees of success. The efforts of some gifted pupils has made the task of establishing which pictures were painted entirely by the masters far from easy.

Tsar Peter the Great of Russia also made his way to Greenwich, and the neighbouring royal dockyard of Deptford, as part of his tour of western Europe in 1697–1699. His reasons for doing so were technical rather than artistic: his mission was to study, collect and copy information on shipbuilding and industrial techniques. He brought craftsmen back to work in Russia, which led to the founding of the modern Russian Navy. As a youth, the tsar had learnt about sailing and seafaring from his friend Franz Timmerman, a Dutch merchant. He owned and sailed many yachts, and his love of yachting was noted by the Prussian ambassador who, writing in 1723, complained that the tsar was 'so occupied with his villas and sailing on the gulf that none has the heart to interrupt him'.

In September 1697, a spectacular mock naval battle took place off Amsterdam in honour of the tsar's arrival. The 'naval ships' were in fact private yachts divided into two squadrons. Peter observed from the flagship of the East India Company. He was apparently so excited by the event that he ordered the captain of his yacht to take part. The Dutch artist Abraham Storck (1644–1710) painted several versions of the occasion (*see page 28*). Like the van de Veldes, he understood the technicalities of the ships he painted. His output was large and popular, and he seems to have employed numerous assistants to turn out 'Storcks', many of which he signed as his own.

Today, it is difficult to envisage yachts taking part in a mock battle but in the seventeenth century it was a popular activity. In 1698, King William III organised a mock naval battle in the Solent, off the Isle of Wight, to mark the visit of Peter the Great. William and his queen, Mary, were both passionate about yachting and made good use of their yachts, notably the *Mary* and the *William and Mary*. One of van de Velde the Younger's most celebrated yachting scenes portrays the *Mary* in 1689 (*see page 29*). Royal enthusiasm for cruising and racing continues to this day and is shared by current members of the Dutch and British royal families. Danish, Norwegian and Spanish royalty are all especially active in international competitive yachting.

THE EMBARKATION OF THE ELECTOR PALATINE AND PRINCESS ELIZABETH IN THE *PRINCE ROYAL* AT MARGATE, 25 APRIL 1613

Adam Willaerts (1577–1664)
(oil on panel, 77.5 x 137cm, dated 1622)
National Maritime Museum, Greenwich.

In February 1613, Princess Elizabeth, daughter of King James I of England and Anne of Denmark, married the head of the German Protestant Union, Frederick, Elector Palatine. The married couple's embarkation at Margate after the wedding was amid scenes of great rejoicing. James I and Anne were in attendance.

The main interest to yachting in this lively picture is not the *Prince Royal*, the large naval ship portrayed broadside on, but the smaller vessel to the left, traditionally identified as the *Disdain*. Although a miniature warship in appearance – she seems to be a small-scale replica of the *Prince Royal* – she is rightly classified as a yacht. She was used by Henry Frederick, Prince of Wales, the eldest son of James I, for cruising, ceremonial and state occasions.

Prince Henry was very fond of yachting, and had commissioned Phineas Pett to build the *Disdain* in 1604 so that he could 'disport himself in above London Bridge'. Pett was a leading member of a family of shipwrights who worked in the royal dockyards and built naval ships and yachts. The Pett family designed several royal yachts during the seventeeth century, including the *Katherine* for Charles II and the *Anne* for his brother James, Duke of York, which famously raced each other on the River Thames in 1661.

Adam Willaerts has captured the sense of joy and pageantry of this historic occasion. Born and trained in Antwerp, Willaerts was the head of a family of artists who painted in the so-called Flemish mannerist tradition. He favoured imaginary compositions showing colourful and animated scenes. However, his marine paintings are often full of nautical detail and he frequently depicts crewmen working the ships. A larger version of this picture is in the British royal collection. The existence of more than one copy suggests that Willaerts' work may have been in demand at the time. It may also indicate that the artist may have had assistants who produced copies of their master's work as part of their training.

THE *BEZAN* YACHT OFF AMSTERDAM

Barent Cornelis Kleeneknecht (1610–1674)
(oil on canvas, 64 x 77cm, circa 1661)
Scheepvaartmuseum, Amsterdam.

Charles II's royal yacht the *Bezan* was launched in 1661 and named after *bezaan*, the Dutch for 'mizzen-sail'. She had a length of 34ft and a beam of 13ft. *Bezan* carried a complement of four, and had the same number of guns for firing signals and salutes. She was broken up in 1687.

Formerly thought to have been painted by Willem van de Velde the Younger, this contemporary portrait of the yacht is in fact by Barent Cornelis Kleeneknecht, an obscure Dutch landscape and marine artist.

THE STERN OF A STATES YACHT

Willem van de Velde the Elder (1611–1693)
(pen and ink on paper, 20.5 x 31.5cm, circa 1680)
National Maritime Museum, Greenwich.

The exquisitely fine and accurate detailing is typical of Willem van de Velde the Elder's drawings. He was one of the finest draughtsmen of maritime subjects. With his eldest son, Willem, they made an outstanding artistic partnership, but they excelled as individuals, too: the Elder as a draughtsman, the Younger as a painter. They worked as roving 'visual journalists', and their drawings and paintings form a significant archive that reveals important historical and technical details of yacht architecture and rigging.

THE YACHT *ROYAL ESCAPE* CLOSE-HAULED IN A BREEZE

Willem van de Velde the Younger (1633–1707)
(oil on canvas, 61 x 73.5cm, circa 1675)
National Maritime Museum, Greenwich.

The *Royal Escape* is one of the earliest recorded royal yachts. In this painting she is shown about to heave-to. The main item of interest to the modern sailor in this little vessel is her mainsail which is set loose-footed and boomless, part-brailed to the spars for stowing or reefing.

The dark step in the foreground of the painting and the low viewpoint were common devices used in the seventeenth century to lead the viewer into the picture and make the scene seem more immediate. Almost two-thirds of the canvas are made up of sky, another hallmark of seventeeth-century Dutch paintings.

A SKETCH OF A SHEER PLAN FOR A YACHT

Willem van de Velde the Younger
(pen and brown ink with grey wash over pencil,
20.3 x 31.3cm, circa 1680)
National Maritime Museum, Greenwich.

As well as painting their patrons' yachts, the van de Veldes may also have sailed their own vessels, too. A series of ten sketch plans reveal that van de Velde the Younger was even designing a yacht for himself, although it is not known if the boat was ever built. The plans depict a characteristically small, Dutch-type bezan yacht, but the style of drawing and the watermarks of the paper suggest that the designs were made shortly after the van de Veldes had settled in England.

A SKETCH OF A SHEER PLAN FOR A YACHT

Willem van de Velde the Younger
(pen and brown ink, 27.5 x 36.3cm, circa 1680)
National Maritime Museum, Greenwich.

Another sketch from van de Velde the Younger's series shows the starboard profile of the yacht the artist was designing. The planned vessel has a relatively large cockpit and a glazed companion hatch leading down two steps into a cabin. The van de Veldes' coat-of-arms is shown at the centre of the elaborate carved decoration over the double doors at the entrance of the hatch.

THE BATTLE OF SCHEVENINGEN, 1653

Willem van de Velde the Elder
(pen-painting on panel, 113.5 x 155.8cm, dated 1655)
National Maritime Museum, Greenwich.

Willem van de Velde the Elder occasionally operated as an official war artist, following first the Dutch and later the English fleets. He can be seen in the foreground, seated sketching in a galliot provided by the Dutch Admiralty during the Battle of Scheveningen, 10 August 1653, the last action of the first Anglo-Dutch War. This painstakingly detailed pen-painting portrays the height of the conflict: the ship on fire is the *Andrew*, flagship of Rear-Admiral Robert Graves. Although the English claimed victory in the battle, during which the Dutch commander-in-chief Marteen Tromp died, their ships were so badly damaged that they had to abandon their blockade of the Dutch coast and return to England to refit.

TWO DUTCH BOEIER YACHTS UNDER SAIL

Willem van de Velde the Elder
(pen-painting on panel, 61 x 84cm, circa 1660)
National Maritime Museum, Greenwich.

In the seventeenth century, the boeier yacht was one of the most popular vessels in the Netherlands for private, recreational yachting. Most of the yachts had elaborate carved work, particularly on the rudderhead. The type has survived almost unchanged to the present day, and boeiers are still a common sight on the country's inland waterways. The recreational nature of the yachts is stressed in this painting by the civilian figures depicted within them. Notice, for example, the helmsman drinking from a flagon in the yacht on the right.

CALM: THE ENGLISH YACHT
PORTSMOUTH
(Detail)

Willem van de Velde the Elder
(oil on canvas, 74.5 x 95.5cm, dated 1675)
National Maritime Museum, Greenwich.

The royal yacht *Portsmouth* is shown here lying at anchor in shallow water and receiving a salute from the ship to its port quarter. The *Portsmouth*, a yacht of eight guns, was built at Woolwich Dockyard in 1674 by Sir Phineas Pett, another member of the Pett shipbuilding family. She was later used as a bomb vessel.

The *Portsmouth* was one of two royal yachts named by King Charles II in honour of his French mistress, Louise de Keroualle. Louise had been introduced to Charles by Louis XIV of France with the intention of her gaining his bed, his confidence and his secrets. She became his mistress in 1671, and within eighteen months she had been created Duchess of Portsmouth, Countess of Fareham and Lady Petersfield. A second royal yacht, the *Fubbs*, launched in 1682, was also named after the king's mistress: Louise had chubby cheeks which led Charles to give her the nickname 'Fubbs'. In seventeenth-century English, 'fubbs' meant 'fat face'. Louise de Keroualle outlived both her yacht namesakes and died in France in 1734, at the age of eighty-five.

ENGLISH ROYAL YACHTS AT SEA

Willem van de Velde the Younger
(oil on canvas, 76 x 99cm, dated 1689)
National Maritime Museum, Greenwich.

Van de Velde the Younger may have intended to portray an actual event in this picture, although to date the yachts in this striking composition have eluded identification. In the left foreground is a royal yacht, possibly the *Cleveland*, viewed from a little before the port beam running before the wind under a mainsail and foresail. A two-decker, flying the royal standard from her mainmast and with her lower ports closed against the rough weather, can be seen in the centre middle-distance. Astern to the right, there are three yachts in line. A ship flying the royal standard could signify that either Charles II or the Duke of York was on board. A possible subject could be the Duke of York's state visit to Scotland in early May 1682. The duke made the journey in the *Gloucester*, escorted by the *Happy Return*, three other ships and five yachts. The *Gloucester* was later wrecked on a sandbank off the Norfolk coast.

A KETCH-RIGGED ROYAL YACHT IN A BREEZE

Johan van der Hagen (1645–c.1720)
(oil on canvas, 45.5 x 40.5cm, circa 1710)
National Maritime Museum, Greenwich.

An unidentified ketch-rigged royal yacht painted in a style reminiscent of Willem van de Velde the Younger. In the early years of the eighteenth century, most English smack-rigged royal yachts were converted to ketch rigs, and all new yachts were built with this rig. The king had around twenty such yachts at his disposal, which were used to convey government servants to the Continent and elsewhere.

Johan van der Hagen's subject matter, technique and palette derive entirely from the van de Veldes. Originally from The Hague, he almost certainly moved to England, where he worked for a time as one of the van de Velde's many studio assistants in Greenwich. His daughter, Bernada, married van de Velde the Younger's son, Cornelis.

REVIEW OF THE DUTCH YACHTS BEFORE TSAR PETER THE GREAT OF RUSSIA AT AMSTERDAM IN 1697

Abraham Storck (1644–1710)
(oil on canvas, 40.5 x 58.5cm, circa 1697)
National Maritime Museum, Greenwich.

The Russian tsar is traditionally believed to be shown on the left side of this picture standing on board a highly decorated yacht identifiable by the flag of the Russian Imperial Eagle. Although some sources believe that Peter merely observed the mock battle, staged by the Dutch in 1697 on what is now the Ijssel Meer, from a distance, others assert that he actually took part in the action.

Abraham Storck, who may have briefly worked in one of the van de Velde's studios, was a superlative painter of marine subjects usually set in his native city of Amsterdam. He excelled at lively quayside and beach scenes with profusions of both craft and people. He also painted fanciful views of imaginary Mediterranean ports, as well as highly accurate sea-fights. Several versions of this picture are recorded. The vessels shown are a mixture of yachts and working boats. Storck is often compared with Ludolf Bakhuizen (1631–1708), a German artist who painted similar subjects, including well-composed portraits of Dutch pleasure craft and States yachts.

THE ROYAL YACHT *MARY* ARRIVING AT GRAVESEND, 12 FEBRUARY 1689

Willem van de Velde the Younger
(oil on canvas, 84 x 127.5cm circa 1689)
National Maritime Museum, Greenwich.

In the centre of this crowded composition is the *Mary*, viewed from before the starboard beam. She was built in 1677 at Chatham Dockyard by Sir Phineas Pett. Flying at her masthead is the special white standard of the Glorious Revolution of 1688 with the legend, 'For the Protestant Religion and the Liberty of England.'

In the foreground, there are several wherries, boats and ships' barges pulling towards the *Mary*. Further away are three state barges also making for the yacht. On the left are two Dutch transport vessels, starboard bow view, tide-rode at anchor and lying close alongside each other. Further away is the *Katherine*. In the background, on the left, the ketch-rigged royal yacht *Fubbs* can be seen. There is a drawing of this picture by Willem van de Velde the Younger in the British royal collection. It names some of the other yachts shown in the background as the *Isabella*, *Anne*, and *Kitchen*.

CHAPTER II

Royal Yachts: *from Sail to Steam*

YACHTS HAVE LONG BEEN USED BY THE BRITISH ROYAL FAMILY FOR STATE OCCASIONS, DIPLOMATIC MISSIONS AND REVIEWS OF THE FLEET, AS WELL AS FOR CRUISING AND RACING. IN MANY CASES, THE YACHTS' NAMES REVEAL THEIR REGAL PEDIGREE: *MARY*, *ROYAL CHARLOTTE*, *ROYAL GEORGE*, *VICTORIA AND ALBERT*, TO NAME BUT A FEW. FOR MORE THAN THREE HUNDRED YEARS, THESE LARGE AND MAJESTIC VESSELS HAVE BEEN AN INSPIRATION TO ARTISTS.

One of the earliest pictures showing King George I's royal yachts was painted in around 1715 by Jan Griffier the Elder (*c.* 1651–1718). In the painting, the artist has depicted the king's principal yachts, including the *Peregrine Galley*, as they are moored on the River Thames off Greenwich (*see page 36*). This particular yacht had originally been used by Queen Anne, and was named after her designer, Peregrine, Lord Danby, who became Marquess of Carmarthen. In 1716, George I renamed the *Peregrine Galley* the *Carolina*.

Originally from Amsterdam, Griffier probably settled in England in 1700. He is known to have owned private yachts, which he may have used as floating studios in which to make sketches for his views of the Thames. In his painting of the *Peregrine Galley* and the other royal yachts, Griffier has shown the magnificent shoreline of the river in great topographical detail. Behind the yachts, the landmarks of Greenwich are clearly visible. Greenwich Hospital, for example, a home for old and disabled seamen, has been captured during its construction. The hospital was founded in 1694, and built to the designs of John Webb, Sir Christopher Wren, Nicholas Hawksmoor and Sir John Vanbrugh. The complex of buildings was not finally completed until the

Previous pages
◆
THE *ROYAL CAROLINE II* AND *KATHERINE*, OFF GREENWICH HOSPITAL PREPARING TO CONVEY KING GEORGE II TO HANOVER, 1752
(Detail)

John Cleveley the Elder (c.1712–1777)
(oil on canvas, 88.9 x 127cm, dated 1752)
Richard Green Galleries.

The *Royal Caroline II* is the larger of the yachts anchored on the River Thames off Greenwich Hospital. She is flying the flag of Lord Anson (1697–1762), who was Admiral of the Fleet and First Lord of the Admiralty. He had personal charge of the royal yachts and was responsible for conveying the king. The *Katherine*, to the left, was a ketch-rigged yacht also built at Deptford and launched on 16 January 1721, weighing 160 tons. Alongside the landing stage at Greenwich Hospital is a royal barge which was built for Frederick, Prince of Wales. The magnificient horse-drawn carriage was used to transport George II. The king made frequent use of his yachts to travel abroad, especially to Hanover.

Cleveley was influenced by Canaletto's dramatic and colourful views of the Thames, and by the accurate harbour scenes of the French painter Claude-Joseph Vernet. Cleveley's art may appear matter-of-fact in comparison with the refinement, flair and dashing brushwork of Canaletto or Vernet, but he enlivened his works with convincing nautical details and with the inclusion of small craft and people going about their everyday business.

1750s. Today, it is home to the Royal Naval College. The Old Royal Observatory, another of Wren's designs, can also be seen in the background.

King George II also used a number of royal yachts, including the *Dorset*, *Drake II*, *Chatham II*, *Plymouth* and the ship-rigged *Royal Caroline II*. The *Royal Caroline II* was built in the Royal Dockyard at Deptford in 1749. She was 90ft in length with a beam of about 25ft, weighed 232 tons, and probably carried a crew of about seventy. She was armed with ten guns, but these were to be used only for ceremonial and state occasions. To commemorate the yacht's launch in 1750, John Cleveley the Elder (*c.*1712–1777), a shipwright in the Deptford dockyard and a self-taught artist, painted the *Royal Caroline II* (*see page 37*). She appears in Cleveley's work on more than one occasion. In his maritime masterpiece, for instance, the artist showed the *Royal Caroline II*, accompanied by a smaller royal yacht, the *Katherine*, off Greenwich Hospital and waiting to receive George II to take him to Hanover (*see pages 30–1*).

In 1761, the *Royal Caroline II* was renamed *Royal Charlotte* in honour of King George III's future queen, Princess Charlotte. The arrival of the princess at Harwich in September of that year was recorded on canvas by the popular French artist Dominic Serres (1722–1793) (*see page 38*). Serres was born near Auch in Gascony and attended the famous English Benedictine school at Douai. To avoid his family's wish for him to become a priest, he ran away to Spain, and then to sea. His ship was captured by the English, however, probably during the Seven Years War. After his release from prison, Serres took advantage of his personal contacts, and used his social skills and charm to earn himself the respect of English society. He eventually achieved considerable commercial success as a marine artist. He became a founder member of the Royal Academy in 1768, and was also appointed marine painter to George III.

Serres was an ardent admirer of the seventeenth-century Dutch marine painters, especially the van de Veldes. After his death, his art collection was sold at the London auctioneers Christie's. It was a remarkable assemblage, containing works by the artists who had influenced him most. The sale included several hundred oil paintings, drawings and prints by the van de Veldes, Simon de Vlieger (*c.* 1600–1653), Claude Lorraine (1600–1682), Jan van de Cappelle (1624–1679), Abraham Storck, Canaletto (1697–1768) and Claude-Joseph Vernet (1714–1789). Serres had also owned pictures by the British artist Charles Brooking (1723–1759), who had taught him art after he arrived in London from France. Serres is known to have copied and adapted a number of Brooking's compositions. This was nothing new: artists had been borrowing from other artistic sources since the earliest times.

Another painter to record Princess Charlotte's arrival in England in 1761 was Richard Wright (1735–1775). This Liverpool-born artist, who shared a studio in London with the celebrated animal painter George Stubbs, produced several versions of the scene. Wright was largely a copyist. In fact, he adapted a picture by Charles Brooking for his composition of the painting, which shows the *Royal Charlotte* and a number of escorting yachts as they battle against rough and stormy conditions. It is known that Wright was sometimes employed by portrait painters to paint maritime subjects in the backgrounds of their own works. For instance, he incorporated the central section of his picture of Princess Charlotte's voyage, a version of which is now held in the National Maritime Museum, into the background of Sir Joshua Reynold's portrait of Mary Panton, Duchess of Ancaster, who had accompanied the princess in the royal yacht *Fubbs*.

Despite the derivative nature of his work, Wright was very popular in his lifetime and was awarded several prizes for his marine and yachting subjects, including three first places in a series of competitions organised by the Society of Arts (now the Royal Society of Arts) in London between 1764 and 1768. The society had launched the competitions as a means of advancing British marine painting.

John Cleveley the Younger (1747–1786) and Robert Cleveley (1747–1809), the twin sons of the elder Cleveley, also painted royal yachts and almost certainly submitted works to the Society of Arts' painting competitions, although they failed to win a prize. They were taught by their father and by the landscape artist and aquatinter Paul Sandby (1730–1809). Robert later specialised in naval battle scenes and became marine painter to the Prince Regent, later King George IV.

One of John Cleveley the Younger's best-known works depicts George III's review of the fleet at Spithead on 22 June 1773. Spithead, a stretch of water lying off the naval base at Portsmouth, on the south coast of England, was the traditional anchorage where the British fleet was reviewed by the sovereign on great occasions and before major battles. In the centre of Cleveley the Younger's picture, drawn in pen and ink and watercolour and now in the National Maritime Museum, is the *Augusta*, the second royal yacht to bear that name, with the royal standard at the main. On board is George III on his way to the review. The king later ordered £350 to be distributed among the crew of the *Augusta*, to mark the event. In the same year, the yacht was renamed *Princess Augusta*. The renaming ceremony was painted by Dominic Serres.

Dominic Serres' eldest son, John Thomas (1759–1825), succeeded his father to the position of marine painter to George III, and was also appointed marine draughtsman to the Admiralty. He was taught by his father and influenced by the theatrical scene painter and artist Philippe-Jacques de Loutherbourg (1740–1812). John Thomas painted several excellent examples of royal yachts, including the *Royal Sovereign* (*see page 39*) and the *Royal George*. He also collaborated on various publications, in particular *Liber Nauticus* and *Instructor in the Art of Marine Drawing*, published by Edward Orme in two parts in 1805 and 1806 and designed to help students draw different types of ships. Unfortunately, his promising career was ruined by a disastrous marriage to a Miss Olivia Wilmot, who believed she was the illegitimate daughter of the Duke of Cumberland, brother of George III. This lost the artist royal favour and plunged him into debt. He eventually died in a debtors' prison in London in 1825.

George IV was an enthusiastic yachtsman, and made use of the *Royal George*, the *Prince Regent* and the *Royal Charlotte II*. The *Royal George* was his principal yacht, and John Thomas Serres recorded the king's arrival in Scotland aboard the vessel in August 1822 (*see page 40*). Serres was almost certainly present at the event.

The return trip was captured in oils by the obscure, though talented, marine painter William Anderson (1757–1837). His *The Return of King George IV to Greenwich from Scotland, 1 September 1822* (*see page 40*) is one of his finest works. Anderson's touches of colour and brushwork may lack the brilliance of Canaletto's similar view of Greenwich, but in certain aspects his painting is a more accurate portrayal of the scene. None of Canaletto's Mediterranean light is found in the work, for example: instead, the rain-filled clouds are more familiar to the British climate. Anderson's highly finished painting style and choice of colouring were based directly on the Dutch marine masters of the seventeenth century, especially the van de Veldes and Ludolf Bakhuizen (1631–1708).

George IV was also active in the sport of yacht racing, and on his ascension to the throne in 1820 he granted the Yacht Club, of which he was patron, the prefix 'Royal'. After George's death in 1830, King William IV succeeded as the Royal Yacht Club's patron, and in 1833 at the behest of Lord Belfast, vice-commodore of the club from 1827 to 1844, he renamed it the Royal Yacht Squadron. William was popularly known as the 'Sailor King', and he made especially good use of the *Royal Adelaide*, a miniature frigate built in 1834. He would often sail her on Virginia Water in Surrey.

When Queen Victoria came to the throne in 1837, she became the patron of the Royal Yacht Squadron. She was more interested in cruising than racing, however. Despite a strong tendency towards seasickness, the queen was an indefatigable traveller. During her long reign, and especially in Prince Albert's lifetime, she made extensive use of the royal yachts to carry her around the coast of Britain and across the Channel to the Continent.

Queen Victoria was the first British monarch to capitalise on the most up-to-date propulsion method of the day: steam. She was fully aware of the promotional value of her yachts and understood that voyaging would raise her profile. Realising her steam yachts were status symbols, she lavished huge fortunes on them.

Queen Victoria's first steam yacht was the *Victoria and Albert*. Designed as a paddle-wheeler by Rear-Admiral Sir William Symonds, she was launched in 1843 to replace George IV's sailing ship the *Royal George*, although that vessel survived until 1905. On *Victoria and Albert*'s maiden voyage, she took the queen and Prince Albert to France. After the construction of the second royal steam yacht *Victoria and Albert II* in 1855, her name was changed to *Osborne*, after Osborne House, the royal residence on the Isle of Wight. She was broken up in 1867.

Victoria and Albert II, the queen's favourite yacht, was also a paddle-wheeler, this time designed by the Controller's Department of the Admiralty. She was built, like her predecessor, at Pembroke in Wales, and was put into commission in April 1855. Of 2,475 tons, she was 300ft in length with a beam of just over 40ft and a draft of 16ft. The yacht remained in service until Victoria's death in December 1901, when was paid off into Dockyard Reserve. She was broken up three years later.

Queen Victoria's third royal steam yacht was launched in May 1899 by the Duchess of York, who later became Queen Mary. *Victoria and Albert III* was a twin-screw steamer with two funnels and three raked masts. She was the largest yacht afloat and her royal apartments were the epitome of grandeur and luxury. Her complement was 367 officers and men and 40 royal servants.

Although most artists preferred to focus on yachts under sail, since they were deemed more visually attractive, the *Victoria and Albert* steam yachts proved popular and lucrative subjects for marine painters, and remain so to this day. Queen Victoria acquired many oil paintings, watercolours, drawings and lithographs of the vessels from a large number of artists, both prominent and obscure. Joseph Miles Gilbert (1799–1876), for example, depicted the *Victoria and Albert* off Spithead in July 1845 in a small oil painting which is now on display in Osborne House. The Hull-born artist William Frederick Settle (1822–1897) also painted a small-scale oil painting, showing various craft, including the *Victoria and Albert II*, with the Isle of Wight in the background (*see page 42*). This picture is now in the National Maritime Museum. One of the most striking images of the royal steam yachts, painted in a semi-impressionist style, was created by the Australian painter Arthur James Weatherall Burgess (1879–1957). In this work, *Victoria and Albert III* is seen from astern, viewed from a steamship during Cowes Week in 1905.

Among the many other artists favoured by Queen Victoria were the amateur marine painters Henry Robins (1820–1892) and Algernon Yockney (1843–1912), a retired Royal Navy paymaster. The Irish painter George Mounsey Wheatley Atkinson (1806–1884), William Adolphus Knell (*c.*1808–1875) (*see page 41*), and the little-known artists Philip Phillips (active 1826–1864), George Housman Thomas (1824–1868), Robert Taylor Pritchett (1828–1907), Robert Thomas Landells (1833–1877), Sydney Prior Hall (1842–1922) and James H C Millar (exhibited 1884–1903) all painted yachting subjects for the queen. These included portraits, races, deck scenes, interior views and formal occasions such as reviews, embarkations and arrivals. Examples of these artists' work can be found in the British royal collection.

The British royal family were not alone in their love of yachts. Royal yachts were used in many European countries including Spain, Portugal, Italy, Sweden, Denmark, Holland, and Germany, as well in the Austro-Hungarian empire. In Sweden, the celebrated naval architect Fredrik Henrik af Chapman (1721–1808) designed several pleasure boats for King Gustaf III and his son, who became Gustaf IV. These included the *Amphion* and the royal barge *Wasaorden*. Chapman's father was a British naval officer who later joined the Royal Swedish Navy. His exquisitely drawn designs of the exterior and interior of vessels are so detailed and carefully arranged that they are works of art in their own right. The profile plans, or drafts, are now in the Krigsarkivet and the Sjöhistoriska Museum, both in Stockholm.

King Louis XIV of France, King Charles II of England's cousin, also showed a keen interest in yachts. Louis XIV's vessels, all called *La Réale*, were designed as richly carved and ornamented galleys. But in terms of seaworthiness they were top heavy and consequently could not be sailed in difficult sea conditions. At the Palace of Versailles, the king created a gigantic sailing pond or *Grand Canal*, as it was known, in which he sailed scaled-down models of naval ships, gondolas, yachts and other craft. Not to by outdone by this extravagance, Charles II had a similar sailing pond constructed in St James's Park, London, in the 1680s.

After Louis XIV's death in 1715, the French monarchs showed little interest in state yachts, and it would be more than one hundred years before the government acquired an official vessel. By this time, there was a great deal more enthusiasm in France for racing than for ceremonial yachts. In 1858, the three-masted single-funnelled paddle-schooner *L'Aigle* was built for Emperor Napoleon III (*see page 43*). Two further yachts followed: the screw barquentine *Jerome Napoléon*, which was launched in 1866 and used for ceremonial and state occasions, and the third and last French imperial yacht, *La Reine Hortense*. She participated in the celebrations during a number of Cowes Weeks during the 1860s, since Napoleon III was a member of the Royal Yacht Squadron. *La Reine Hortense* was lithographed in colours by L le Breton, after an original design by Frédéric Roux (1805–1870), a member of a famous family of ship portraitists from Marseilles. The Roux family are popular with watercolour enthusiasts and collectors today because of their attention to nautical detail. A number of maritime museums own works by the family, including the National Maritime Museum and the Peabody Museum of Salem, Massachusetts.

Kaiser Wilhelm II of Germany owned four yachts named *Meteor*, and these made notable appearances at the Kiel and Cowes regattas. For cruising, the kaiser used the paddle-schooner *Hohenzollern*, built in 1893. He also had use of the *Royal Louise*, a sailing frigate that King William IV had presented to Frederick William III of Germany. But the kaiser was not satisfied with these and he took charge of a new yacht, also called *Hohenzollern*, which had originally been intended as a German Admiralty dispatch vessel. The old *Hohenzollern* was renamed *Kaiseradler*. In 1905, Wilhelm II presented a gold cup for a transatlantic race. The race attracted eleven entries, and was won by the American schooner *Atlantic* in the record time of twelve days, four hours and one minute. With the arrival of the First World War, and increased anti-German sentiment, the cup was smashed on the stage of the Metropolitan Opera House, upon which it was discovered that the trophy was in fact made of lead covered with a thin coat of gold. Bullets were made from the cup so that it could be fired back at the kaiser.

The award for the most bizarre royal yacht design belongs to Tsar Alexander II of Russia's triple-screw steam yacht *Livadia*. Built by the Govan yard in Scotland in 1880, and sumptuously fitted out like a floating palace, she was almost circular. Although she was a very comfortable and successful yacht, she was hardly ever used and was broken up in 1926.

THE ROYAL YACHT
THE *PEREGRINE GALLEY* AND
OTHER VESSELS OFF GREENWICH

Jan Griffier the Elder (c.1651–1718)
(oil on canvas, 114.5 x 178cm, circa 1715)
National Maritime Museum, Greenwich.

The *Peregrine Galley*, portrayed broadside on, was built in 1700 and later
renamed the *Carolina* in 1716. She was the principal yacht of King George I, and
was also used by George II. George I also made use of many other yachts, including *Chatham*, *Queenborough II*, *Katherine III*, *Fubbs III* and *Mary III*.

At first, Jan Griffier the Elder specialised in flower painting, but he later turned
towards architectural and topographical subjects. He was also an accomplished car-
tographer. According to Colonel Maurice Harold Grant, author of *A Chronological
History of Old English Landscape Painters*, the artist's attempt to sail to Rotterdam in
his private yacht ended in disaster. He lost the yacht and with it most of his savings.
Undeterred, he immediately built another vessel and returned to England.

Royal Caroline Yacht.

THE ROYAL YACHT *ROYAL CAROLINE II*

John Cleveley the Elder (c.1712–1777)
(oil on canvas, 80 x 110cm, dated 1750)
National Maritime Museum, Greenwich.

The ship-rigged *Royal Caroline II* was designed as a luxury cruising and transportation yacht by the Surveyor of the Navy, Mr Joseph Allin. She was named after Queen Caroline, wife of King George II, and was the second yacht of that name. John Cleveley may well have assisted with the decoration and painting of the yacht's head and stern galleries. He painted the *Royal Caroline II* in 1750 to commemorate her launch at Deptford on 29 January of that year.

John Cleveley had originally worked as a joiner in the Royal Dockyard at Deptford, before turning to full-time painting. From 1747 to the mid-1750s, he produced a series of paintings of ship launches at Deptford. Among his favourite subjects were royal yachts and the pomp and pageantry of regal occasions. His earlier trade had given him an intimate knowledge of many different kinds of vessels, enabling him to render his subjects with great detail and accuracy.

THE ARRIVAL OF PRINCESS CHARLOTTE AT HARWICH, 1761

Dominic Serres (1722–1793)
(oil on canvas, 81.5 x 129.5cm, dated 1763)
National Maritime Museum, Greenwich.

In 1761, the *Royal Caroline II* was sumptuously refitted and renamed the *Royal Charlotte*. In September of that year, the *Royal Charlotte*, accompanied by the royal yachts *Mary*, *Katherine* and *Fubbs*, received Princess Charlotte of Mecklenburg-Strelitz, the future queen consort, on her arrival from Kiel. The princess was delighted with the salutes, the cannon-fire and the bell-ringing, exclaiming 'Am I worthy of all these honours?'

In this charming painting, Dominic Serres has brilliantly captured the scene of the princess's arrival at Harwich. At first glance, the picture may appear to be unrelated to yachting, but in fact Serres has imaginatively highlighted the *Royal Charlotte*, as she passes Landguard Fort, by using shafts of radiant light. The artist has caught something of the pageantry and spectacle of this regal occasion by making a feature of the expansive stretch of foreground landscape and by including the fashionable quayside strollers. The style of the preparatory drawing for this picture, now in the National Maritime Museum, Greenwich, suggests that Serres may have been taught by the watercolourist and aquatinter Paul Sandby.

KING GEORGE III ABOARD THE *ROYAL SOVEREIGN* OFF WEYMOUTH IN 1806

John Thomas Serres (1759–1825)
(oil on canvas, 137 x 167.5cm, dated 1809)
National Maritime Museum, Greenwich.

The elegant proportions of the ship-rigged *Royal Sovereign*, the largest and fastest yacht of her day, are contrasted with the quayside activity and the workaday boats of the foreground. The royal yacht was built in 1804 and named after George III. Her interiors were fitted out with 'velvets, damasks, satins and mahogany paneling'. From 1832, she was used as a depot ship. She was broken up in 1850.

The master mariner turned marine painter Nicholas Pocock (1740–1821) also painted a portrait of the *Royal Sovereign*. Pocock's painting, which is now held in the National Maritime Museum, Greenwich, portrays the royal yacht as she conveys the exiled Louis XVIII from England to France on 24 April 1814. Louis was returning home to ascend the French throne after the defeat of Napoleon.

THE ARRIVAL OF HIS MAJESTY GEORGE IV IN SCOTLAND ABOARD THE *ROYAL GEORGE*, ACCOMPANIED BY THE ROYAL FLOTILLA, AUGUST 1822

John Thomas Serres
(pen and ink and watercolour, 33.2 x 89.8cm, circa 1822)
National Maritime Museum, Greenwich.

To the left of the group of vessels, the royal yacht *Royal George*, which was launched in 1817, flies the royal standard from her mainmast. She is being towed by a steam vessel.

John Thomas Serres was equally adept in oils and watercolour. In his capacity as marine draughtsman to the Admiralty he would sail aboard naval vessels to record coastlines and topographical details. Examples of his coastal profiles can be found in a publication entitled *The Little Sea Torch*, published in 1801.

HER MAJESTY'S VISIT TO THE FLAGSHIP, 11 AUGUST 1853

William Adolphus Knell (c.1808–1875)
(watercolour and body colour, 25 x 41cm, circa 1853)
National Maritime Museum, Greenwich.

Queen Victoria went on board HMS *Duke of Wellington* during a review of the fleet in August 1853. The paddle box of the *Victoria and Albert*, the first of that name, appears on the extreme left. To the left of centre is the flagship, the *Duke of Wellington*, and steaming to the right is the royal yacht *Fairy*, active between 1844 and 1868.

It is believed that William Adolphus Knell was based in London and that William Callcott Knell (*c.*1830–*c.*1876), also a marine painter, was his son. They exhibited some paintings at the Royal Academy, although their work is invariably of uneven quality.

THE RETURN OF KING GEORGE IV TO GREENWICH FROM SCOTLAND, 1 SEPTEMBER 1822

William Anderson (1757–1837)
(oil on canvas, 75 x 108cm, circa 1822)
National Maritime Museum, Greenwich.

George IV was the first sovereign to visit Scotland since Charles II. This picture shows him being rowed to the watergate at Greenwich from his yacht the *Royal George*, the large three-mast vessel shown at anchor, starboard broadside view. In the right foreground is the Lord Mayor's barge, complete with orchestra. The Greenwich Hospital buildings (now the Royal Naval College) are lined with pensioners as well as children from the Naval Asylum School.

Little is known of William Anderson except that he was born in Scotland and that he became a shipwright. By the late 1780s, he had settled in London. Anderson first exhibited at the Royal Academy in 1787, and at the British Institution in 1810. It is traditionally believed that he collaborated with the landscape painter Julius Caeser Ibbetson. Anderson died in the year Queen Victoria came to the throne.

THE ROYAL YACHT *VICTORIA AND ALBERT II*

William Frederick Settle (1822–1897)
(oil on panel, 20.5 x 29cm, dated 1867)
National Maritime Museum, Greenwich.

Although the *Victoria and Albert II* can be seen on the far left of this small-scale painting, she is not the main focus of the picture. In the foreground is a small yacht of the Royal Yacht Squadron, while to the right is a 51-gun British frigate, the *Immortalité*. Beyond these vessels lies the famous *Warrior*, the first British ironclad ship, launched in 1860 and now on display in Portsmouth. The Isle of Wight is visible in the background.

Settle was drawing master of the Hull Mechanics' Institute, but in 1863 he moved to London. He gave Queen Victoria instruction in drawing and she, in return, commissioned him to design nautical Christmas cards. He was associated with several British yacht clubs. Settle's contemporary, George Mears (active 1860–1895) also painted royal and racing yachts with such regularity it is thought that he was one of Queen Victoria's official marine artists.

THE ROYAL DUTCH PADDLE STEAMER *DE LEEUW*

Nineteenth-Century Dutch School
(watercolour, 60.5 x 91.8cm, circa 1850)
Scheepvaartmuseum, Amsterdam.

Although the Dutch royal family displayed a keen interest in yachts powered by sail, they also owned a number of steam yachts. One of their favourites was the paddle-steamer *De Leeuw*, which was launched in 1827 and lasted fifty-five years, before being replaced by the paddle-schooner *De Valk* in 1882. King William II of the Netherlands, who was a member of the Royal Yacht Squadron, brought *De Valk* to Cowes on several occasions. In appearance, both yachts were widely regarded as 'ugly ducklings'.

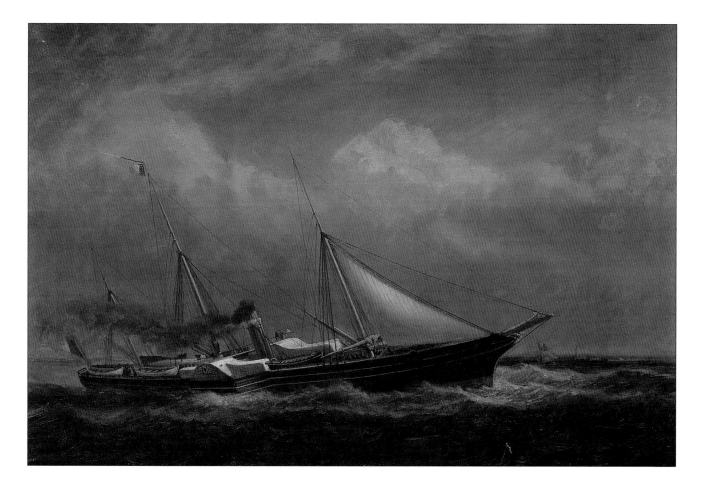

THE FRENCH IMPERIAL YACHT *L'AIGLE*

Adolphe Couveley (1805–1867)
(oil on canvas,
54.5 x 80cm, circa 1860)
Cliché Musée de la Marine, Paris.

L'Aigle, with Empress Eugénie aboard, led the procession of ships during the opening of the Suez Canal in 1869.

Adolphe Couveley, or Couvelet, was based in Le Havre, in Normandy, Northern France. According to Bénézit's dictionary of artists, Couveley was a keen traveller and made trips to Turkey, Greece and England. He became a director of the Le Havre Museum and exhibited at the Paris Salon from 1834 to 1866.

CHAPTER III

Yacht Racing:
the Quest for Speed

Tʜᴇ ʀᴏʏᴀʟ ꜰᴀᴍɪʟʏ'ꜱ ᴀꜱꜱᴏᴄɪᴀᴛɪᴏɴ ᴡɪᴛʜ ʏᴀᴄʜᴛɪɴɢ ʜᴇʟᴘᴇᴅ ᴘʀᴏᴍᴏᴛᴇ ᴛʜᴇ ꜱᴘᴏʀᴛ ᴀᴍᴏɴɢ ᴛʜᴇ Bʀɪᴛɪꜱʜ ᴜᴘᴘᴇʀ ᴄʟᴀꜱꜱᴇꜱ, ᴀɴᴅ ʙʏ ᴛʜᴇ ᴇɴᴅ ᴏꜰ ᴛʜᴇ ᴇɪɢʜᴛᴇᴇɴᴛʜ ᴄᴇɴᴛᴜʀʏ, ɪᴛ ᴡᴀꜱ ᴀɴ ᴀᴄᴛɪᴠɪᴛʏ ᴇɴᴊᴏʏᴇᴅ ʙʏ ʟᴀʀɢᴇ ɴᴜᴍʙᴇʀꜱ ᴏꜰ ᴡᴇᴀʟᴛʜʏ ᴀʀɪꜱᴛᴏᴄʀᴀᴛꜱ ᴀɴᴅ ʙᴜꜱɪɴᴇꜱꜱᴍᴇɴ. Mᴀɴʏ ᴏꜰ ᴛʜᴇꜱᴇ ꜰᴏʀᴍᴇᴅ ᴄʟᴜʙꜱ ᴀɴᴅ ᴏʀɢᴀɴɪꜱᴇᴅ ʀᴀᴄᴇꜱ. Aꜱ ᴄᴏᴍᴘᴇᴛɪᴛɪᴏɴꜱ ʙᴇᴄᴀᴍᴇ ꜰɪᴇʀᴄᴇʀ ᴀɴᴅ ꜰɪᴇʀᴄᴇʀ, ᴏᴡɴᴇʀꜱ ʟᴏᴏᴋᴇᴅ ꜰᴏʀ ɴᴇᴡ ᴡᴀʏꜱ ᴛᴏ ᴍᴀᴋᴇ ᴛʜᴇɪʀ ʏᴀᴄʜᴛꜱ ꜰᴀꜱᴛᴇʀ.

Two of the most famous yacht clubs were founded in the eighteenth century. The world's oldest club is the Water Club of the Harbour of Cork in Ireland. It is now believed that it was one of Charles II's courtiers, the first Earl of Inchiquin, who popularised the sport in Cork. Whether or not this is true, what is certain is that by 1720 the earl's great-grandson, William O'Brien, the 6th Lord Inchiquin, and five friends collectively formed the Water Club of the Harbour of Cork. A pair of pictures showing the club's fleet (*see page 49*) were painted in 1738 by the London-born artist Peter Monamy (1681–1749), and later presented to the club by the Marquis of Thomond, a member during the club's revival in 1806.

The first yacht club to be established in England, and the second oldest club in the world, was the Cumberland Sailing Society, founded in 1775 by George III's brother, Henry Frederick, Duke of Cumberland. Its members participated in regular sailing regattas along the River Thames above Blackfriars Bridge. After violent disagreements at the race held in 1823, some members of the society broke away and in 1830 formed the Thames Yacht Club under the patronage of King William IV. Now known as the Royal Thames Yacht Club, it has its clubhouse in Knightsbridge, London.

Previous pages
◆
PILOT CUTTERS RACING TO A SHIP
(Detail)

Admiral Richard Brydges Beechey (1808–1895)
(oil on canvas, 92.5 x 138.5cm, dated 1873)
National Maritime Museum, Greenwich.

This painting depicts a workaday race. As soon as the pilot jack was raised at the foremast of a merchantman, the signal was given for the pilot cutters to race to the ship. Only the first pilot aboard would be paid for his service. Not surprisingly, pilot rigs were constantly developed to increase speed and were copied by yacht designers. The celebrated schooner yacht *America* was designed along the lines of a New York pilot cutter. The *Jolie Brise*, winner of the first Fastnet race, run on 15 August 1925, was a converted Le Havre pilot cutter.

Beechey was the youngest son of the celebrated portrait painter Sir William Beechey RA, and was one of the most accomplished naval officer artists. In 1821, he enrolled at the Royal Naval College in Portsmouth, where he would have been taught by John Christian Schetky. During the following year, he went to sea. Four years later, Beechey served as a midshipman on HMS *Blossom*, which was commanded by his brother Captain Frederick Beechey, and embarked on a three-year voyage of discovery in the Pacific.

In spite of the growing interest in yacht racing, images of the sport from this early period are extremely rare. Royal and state occasions were still by far the most popular yachting subjects for artists. There are a few exceptions, however. One example is a small-scale oil painting by Francis Swaine (*c*.1715–1782) showing yachts of the Cumberland Sailing Society racing on the Thames off Lambeth Palace in the year of the club's formation (*see page 51*). Another racing scene, painted by Daniel Turner in around 1782, shows several of the club's gaff-rigged yachts ploughing through the river above Blackfriars. The yachts dominate the scene, dwarfing all the other craft on the water and even the surrounding buildings, including St Paul's Cathedral.

Dominic Serres painted the earliest recorded image of a regatta off Cowes in 1776 (*see page 52*). Although the event has not been identified, it indicates that yacht racing was taking place at Cowes at least forty years before the formal establishment of a yacht club there. The diarist and topographical artist Joseph Farington (1747–1821) also depicted a regatta off Cowes in 1794 (*see page 53*).

Around this time, however, yachting in Britain's coastal waters was becoming increasingly hazardous as a consequence of the country's war with France. It was not until 1815, when the defeat of Napoleon restored peace to Europe, that British yachtsmen could once again enjoy safe and unrestricted cruising, sailing and competitive racing.

This was the beginning of the golden age of yachting. During the course of the nineteenth century, with the increasing prosperity of the middle classes, the sport would reach unprecedented heights of popularity.

Many new yacht clubs were formed and some of the world's most famous races were run for the first time. In particular it was the establishment of the Yacht Club at Cowes in 1815, later the Royal Yacht Squadron, that encouraged the growth of British yachting. At the club's spring meeting in 1826, it was unanimously resolved that 'a gold cup of the value of £100 be sailed for by vessels belonging to the club, of any rig or tonnage'. This first historic race led to no less than six cups being offered in the following year.

The establishment of the Yacht Club at Cowes also acted as a catalyst for the development of yachting art. Until this time, portraits of specific yachts were relatively rare. Although there were plenty of paintings with yachts in the composition, the vessels themselves were not normally the principal focus of the work. Often, the real subject of the painting was the event itself – a royal review, a ceremonial arrival, or a regatta – rather than the individual yachts taking part. The close attention given to topographical detail by artists such as Jan Griffier the Elder and John Cleveley the Elder suggests that the yachts appearing in their paintings were often merely elements in a landscape scene. In fact, in the late eighteenth century, the Royal Academy barely considered marine painting, never mind yachting art, a separate genre at all, simply a category of landscape, a comparatively minor art. Of the academy's thirty-six founder members, Dominic Serres was the only professional marine painter.

By around 1830, however, yachting art had emerged as a specialist genre, and many more artists were able to make a living by painting yachts or yacht races. Proud individual yacht owners were eager to commission artists to paint portraits of their favourite yachts and to commemorate their racing triumphs, or perhaps heroic failures. The Royal Yacht Squadron went one step further, and in 1828 appointed John Christian Schetky (1778–1874) as their first honorary painter. He held this position until 1858. The appointment continues to this day and is currently held by David Cobb (b.1921), a past president of the British Royal Society of Marine Artists.

John Christian Schetky was also marine painter in ordinary to George IV, William IV and Queen Victoria. The artist's attendance was required on diplomatic and state occasions and for reviews of the fleet at Spithead. Queen Victoria and her family delighted in his ability to make rapid on-the-spot sketches. Schetky collaborated with Lord John Manners on a splendid visual record of a cruise around the Scottish coasts in 1848 in the 93-ton yacht *Resolution*. His original designs were lithographed by J Needham and published in *Sketches and Notes of a Cruise in Scotch Waters on Board His Grace the Duke of Rutland's Yacht* Resolution *in the Summer of 1848*.

The demands of yacht owners dictated the form that yachting art would take. Customers wanted an accurate record of their vessel. They wanted above all precise nautical detail: the shape of the hull, the arrangement of the masts, rigging and positioning of the sails all had to be convincing. In most cases, the artist showed the yacht broadside on so that more of the vessel could be seen and more attention could be given to its detail. This remained the preferred format for yacht portraits until well into the twentieth century, unless the owner stipulated otherwise. Other vessels were often introduced to visually enhance the composition and emphasise the scale of the yacht in focus. The sea and landscape were usually secondary to the yacht itself, although later in the nineteenth century there was an increasing demand for pictures that combined both nautical detail and naturalistic effects.

In the yachting art of this period, it is often difficult to distinguish working boats from racing yachts. This is not surprising because the design of many gaff-rigged working vessels, such as pilot cutters and smugglers' boats, which were designed to be fast under sail, were ideally suited for yachting. Yacht owners looked towards the construction of these boats to try to improve the performance of their own vessels. The Marquis of Anglesey, for example, commissioned Philip Sainty, a well-known builder of smugglers' boats and a smuggler himself, to construct the cutter yacht *Pearl*. When the *Pearl* was launched in 1820, she was one of the fastest yachts of her day. Other successful yachts were based on the design of the fast gaff-rigged cutter, too. They included Lord Belfast's *Harriet* of 96 tons and the most celebrated of all British royal racing yachts, the *Britannia*, built in 1893 by G L Watson.

Not only was the gaff rig the most efficient racing rig for the best part of a century, but its quadrilateral form and imposing topsails were also a great inspiration to artists. Admiral Richard Brydges Beechey (1808–1895), for example, painted a dramatic composition showing two gaff-rigged pilot cutters racing to an incoming ship (*see pages 44–5*); John Christian Schetky captured the Marquis of Anglesey's *Pearl* in a painting that is now part of the Royal Yacht Squadron's collection (*see page 53*); and Dominic Serres, Thomas Whitcombe (*c.*1752–1824) and William John

Huggins (1781–1845) all portrayed fast gaff-rigged working yachts, such as revenue cutters and Trinity House craft (*see page 52*).

Huggins painted a wide range of maritime subjects, including racing yacht portraits and regattas, although he is best known for his portraits of East and West Indiamen. He benefited from a large number of patrons and had excellent contacts in yachting circles. The printmaker C Rosenburg aquatinted several yachting designs prepared by Huggins, including the Earl of Yarborough's ship-rigged yacht *Falcon* of 351 tons. Yarborough was the first commodore of the Yacht Club at Cowes. In 1827, Lord Belfast commissioned Huggins to paint his cutter yacht *Harriet* to commemorate his appointment as vice-commodore of the club. In 1847, Lord Belfast succeeded the Earl of Yarborough to become commodore. Huggins' picture is now on display in the Royal Yacht Squadron.

Huggins also worked in partnership with his son-in-law, the aquatinter Edward Duncan (1803–1882). Huggins would provide maritime designs which Duncan would translate into prints. Duncan collaborated with many other marine artists, too, including the Scottish painter William Clark of Greenock (1803–1883). One of their finest yachting prints depicts yachts of the Royal Northern Yacht Club at a regatta in Rothesay Bay in around 1830. Duncan usually worked on a small scale, and occasionally painted yacht portraits in oils. These paintings are remarkable for their clarity of design and atmospheric effects.

At the beginning of the twentieth century, small racing yachts in Britain began to use the Bermudian rig rather than the gaff rig. The widespread adoption of this form of rig, a triangular sail set on a single mast, was a major development for yachting. By using taller trees to make longer masts and doing away with the heavy gaff, a lighter rig could be achieved. This in turn led to even longer masts and a greater sail area. A small crew could handle the rig and it was an efficient sail plan, especially when sailing to windward.

The origin of the Bermudian rig remains obscure. Having commonly been used by sailing craft in the West Indies from around 1800, it was introduced for small racing craft in Britain from about 1911, and later adopted by larger yachts between the two world wars. One of the first big cutters to adopt the Bermudian rig was the *Nyria*, originally built as a 23-metre vessel under the International Rule. She adopted the Bermudian rig in the 1920s.

Nyria was portrayed by the British poster designer and marine painter Charles Pears (1873–1958) racing off Cowes in summer 1923.

Images of Bermudian sailing vessels in the early part of the nineteenth century are rare. One striking example was painted by John Lynn (active 1830s–1860s) (*see page 56*). Lynn was based in London and submitted work to the Suffolk Street Galleries of the Society of British Artists, a group of rebel artists. He had extensive contacts with naval officers and yacht clubs which kept him supplied with regular commissions. Some of his pictures were engraved. Several of Lynn's contemporaries, including J F Argent, Henry Sargeant and an obscure painter who signed himself Horton, all of whom were active between the 1830s and 1860s, also carved a niche for themselves as marine painters with a special interest in yachting.

Of these artists, Henry Sargeant is the most noteworthy. He worked in Portsmouth, although he also spent time on the Isle of Wight painting yachts of the Royal Yacht Squadron. He probably lived with John Nash, the renowned London architect, during his painting trips to the island. It is believed that he was official marine painter to Queen Adelaide, wife of William IV. One of his pictures, depicting the government cutter yacht *Emerald* cruising in Osborne Bay (*see page 57*) has the royal stamp of William IV, as well as the inventory stamp of Queen Victoria, on its reverse.

Charles Gregory (1810–1896) and his son George (1849–1938) also painted for members of the Royal Yacht Squadron. Charles Gregory's work has been mistaken for that of the American artist Archibald Cary Smith (1837–1911). In a marine sale in June 1988, a leading London auction house sold a painting attributed to Charles Gregory. Subsequent cleaning, however, revealed the signature 'A Cary Smith'. Cary Smith painted a variety of yachting subjects, and exhibited regularly at the National Academy in New York. He also later became a distinguished yacht designer. The skills needed to produce paintings with exacting nautical detail were very useful to a designer. Perhaps Cary's best-known yacht was *Mischief*, the defender and winner of the America's Cup challenge in 1881. This particular competition thrilled the rapidly growing yacht-loving public in the second half of the nineteenth century. It also captured the imagination of yachting artists, and to this day the America's Cup races, and the schooner yacht *America* herself, remain popular yachting subjects.

YACHTS OF THE WATER CLUB OF THE HARBOUR OF CORK, 1738

TOP
Peter Monamy (1681–1749)
(oil on canvas, 56 x 65cm, circa 1738)
Royal Cork Yacht Club.

BOTTOM
Peter Monamy
(oil on canvas, 69 x 89cm, circa 1738)
Royal Cork Yacht Club.

During the 1830s, the Water Club of the Harbour of Cork changed its name several times and also received the prefix, 'Royal'. These companion pictures were presented to what is now called the Royal Cork Yacht Club by the Marquis of Thomond, a member of the club. Sir Thomas Lipton was among the club's most prominent members in the twentieth century.

Monamy was one of the earliest British marine painters of note. His style was indebted to the work of the van de Veldes, whose paintings he studied, copied and adapted. He styled himself, 'Peter Monamy/Painter of ships and marine prospects/Second only to van de Velde'. Monamy specialised in naval actions and general shipping scenes. He also painted yachting pictures, including portraits of royal yachts.

THE FLEET OF THE CUMBERLAND SAILING SOCIETY RACING ON THE THAMES

Daniel Turner (active 1782-1801)
(oil on canvas, 44 x 60cm, circa 1782)
Royal Thames Yacht Club.

Yachts of the Cumberland Sailing Society are shown here racing along a stretch of the River Thames above Blackfriars Bridge in 1782. The vessels are of various sizes and all of them are gaff-rigged. Turner, a topographical landscape painter and printmaker, has captured the speed, movement and excitement of yacht racing in this painting, which may have been based on an eye-witness account. Wren's architectural masterpiece, St Paul's Cathedral, is clearly visible in the background.

THE YACHT RACE ON THE THAMES FOR THE DUKE'S CUP, 1775

Francis Swaine (c.1715–1782)
(oil on panel, 13.5 x 22cm, circa 1775)
Royal Thames Yacht Club.

The Duke of Cumberland was so enthusiastic about the sport of yachting that he gave a 'silver cup to be sailed for on Thursday 11 July 1775, from Westminster Bridge to Putney Bridge and back by pleasure sailing boats from two to five tons burden, and constantly lying above London Bridge'.

The free handling of paint in this lively small panel picture suggests that it was painted on the spot. The artist worked in London and had first-hand experience of the sea. He painted general shipping and battle scenes, and won the second prize of fifteen guineas in the first marine painting competition organised by the Society of Arts in 1764. Swaine was influenced by the work of Charles Brooking and Peter Monamy, after whom he named his son, Monamy Swaine, who was also a marine painter.

YACHTS OF THE CUMBERLAND SAILING SOCIETY RACING ON THE THAMES

William Havell (1782–1857)
(oil on canvas, 49.5 x 70cm, circa 1815)
National Maritime Museum, Greenwich.

The Thames remained the centre of yachting until the mid-Victorian period, by which time the river was becoming dirty and congested as London grew into the world's largest port. Yachtsmen became disillusioned with having their races interrupted by steamers and barges and so, by using the new railways, they travelled to the Solent on the south coast of England to practise their sport.

Note the dark step in the foreground of the painting. As in van de Velde the Younger's depiction of *Royal Escape* (*see page 21*), the artist has used this device to lead the viewer into the picture space.

Details of William Havell are scant. He was a landscape painter in a style reminiscent of John Constable. His studio sale was held at the auctioneers Christie's in the year after his death.

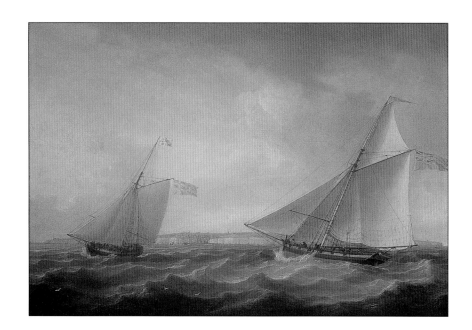

A TRINITY HOUSE YACHT AND A REVENUE CUTTER OFF RAMSGATE

Thomas Whitcombe (c.1752–1824)
(oil on canvas, 61 x 91.5cm, circa 1810)
National Maritime Museum, Greenwich.

At first glance, it appears that this picture shows yachts racing. In fact, to the right is a cutter of the Revenue Service. Revenue cutters were single-masted and gaff-rigged. They were designed expressly to prevent smuggling and enforcing customs regulations. Speed was of paramount importance and led to their special design, which was subsequently copied by yacht designers. On the left of this painting, a Trinity House yacht flies the distinctive jack of that institution, composed of the red cross of St George between four ships. Trinity House was established by Henry VIII as a guild of 'shipmen and mariners' of England and remains to this day responsible for the lighthouses, lightships and navigational marker buoys around Britain's coasts.

Whitcombe was a prodigious recorder of the naval battles of the French Revolutionary Wars. Apart from fifty paintings that were reproduced in print form in *The Naval Achievements of Great Britain*, published in 1819, the artist produced at least one hundred wartime paintings that were also engraved, as well as painting more peaceful subjects. He exhibited at the Royal Academy between 1783 and 1824. His ability to draw the stance of ships in correct relationship to the elements, and his atmospheric use of strongly patterned clouds and seas full of movement, suggest that he had some first-hand experience of the ocean. At its best, Whitcombe's mature work is crisp and fresh, but it is most valuable as an historical record.

A REGATTA OFF COWES WITH NAVAL CUTTERS

Dominic Serres (1722–1793)
(oil on canvas, 61 x 100.5cm, dated 1776)
Royal Yacht Squadron.

This painting of 1776 clearly demonstrates that yacht races were taking place off Cowes before the formal establishment of the Yacht Club in 1815. Its name was changed in July 1833 when William IV, the 'Sailor King', expressed the wish that it should be known as the Royal Yacht Squadron.

Serres' composition is reminiscent of his earlier oil painting *The Arrival of Princess Charlotte at Harwich, 1761* (see page 38). He was a gifted, although invariably prosaic, recorder of maritime subjects. In the last year of his life, he held the prestigious appointment of librarian to the Royal Academy. His impressive painting showing George III reviewing the fleet at Spithead in 1778 is now in the British royal collection. Serres' youngest son, Dominic Junior (*c.*1761–1804) was also a marine painter.

A TRINITY HOUSE REGATTA
OFF COWES IN 1794

Joseph Farington (1747–1821)
(pen and ink and wash on paper,
22 x 101.5cm, dated 1794)
Royal Yacht Squadron.

This rare panoramic work shows a yachting scene that was almost certainly witnessed by the artist. The painting is framed in oak from the royal yacht the *Royal George*. Farington is better known for his diary, which he wrote between 1793 and 1821 and which is the prime source of information on the arts in London of that period. Farington was a skilful topographical draughtsman capable of highly atmospheric work, which he regularly exhibited at the Royal Academy in London. He collaborated with the marine artist Nicholas Pocock (1741–1821) on a remarkable series of canvases of the major naval ports of Britain, now in the National Maritime Museum, Greenwich.

LORD ANGLESEY'S
CUTTER YACHT
PEARL

John Christian Schetky (1778–1874)
(oil on canvas, 56 x 75cm, circa 1830)
Royal Yacht Squadron.

Pearl was built by Philip Sainty, an established boat builder and well-known smuggler, based at Wivenhoe, Essex. His reputation for designing fast boats prompted Lord Anglesey to procure the release of Sainty, his brother and brother-in-law from prison. Sainty had imposed this as a condition before he agreed to start work on Anglesey's yacht.

Schetky was born in Edinburgh. His family was of Hungarian origin, his father a musician and composer, his mother an amateur artist. He served briefly aboard the frigate HMS *Hind* before turning to marine painting. He was an excellent teacher and was professor of drawing at the Royal Naval Academy in Portsmouth (1811–1836), where he taught trainee naval officers. Schetky's own paintings, although highly competent in terms of draughtsmanship and atmospheric effects, are often lacking in colour, hence his nickname 'Old Sepia'. After his death at the age of ninety-five, Schetky's daughter wrote his biography, *Ninety Years of Work and Play*.

HMS *PICKLE II* OFF PORT ROYAL, JAMAICA

William John Huggins (1781–1845)
(oil on canvas, 46 x 61cm, dated 1841)
The Kelton Foundation Collection.

Previously believed to be a yacht of the Royal Yacht Squadron, this vessel has now been identified as the British schooner *Pickle II*, built in 1827. Her rig and lines could easily have been mistaken for those of a yacht. She relayed orders, carried dispatches and dignitaries and was also used as an advance scout. Her size and rig enabled her to outmanoevre enemy ships. It is thought that the white dress of the crew would have been Pusser's issue. The Pusser was responsible on board naval ships for the provision of food and clothing.

Huggins spent several years at sea with the East India Company, before taking up marine painting. His work is characterised by a creamy palette and fluid brushwork. The artist was popular with seafarers because he had an intimate knowledge of ships. Huggins exhibited at the Royal Academy and in 1836 was appointed marine painter to William IV. Not everyone was an admirer of his work, however. The outspoken Victorian art critic John Ruskin thought his portrayals of ships moving through the water lacked authenticity.

COME TO GRIEF

Admiral Richard Brydges Beechey
(oil on canvas, 61 x 91.5cm, dated 1879)
N R Omell Gallery.

This painting shows yachts racing off the Irish coast. Beechey was fascinated by ships and small craft battling against the elements or in distress. The yacht in the foreground has most certainly come to grief, having lost part of her mainmast overboard. She is not going to win the race. Most of Beechey's yachting subjects were rendered on commission, notably the steam yacht *Wanderer*, which the artist painted for her owner and master C J Lambert in 1883. In the same year, the painting was translated into a wood engraving for C J and S Lambert's *The Voyage of The Wanderer*, published by Macmillan & Co, which recorded the vessel's recent two-year world voyage.

A Bermudian Schooner Yacht off Port Royal, Jamaica

John Lynn (active 1830s–1860s)
(oil on canvas, 30 x 45cm, dated 1834)
National Maritime Museum, Greenwich.

The flag codes of the schooner yacht identify the vessel as belonging to the Royal Yacht Squadron. The Bermudian rig was commonly used by sailing craft in and around the West Indies from about 1800. It was introduced for small racing craft in Britain from about 1911 and later adopted by larger yachts between the two world wars.

Biographical details of the London-based artist John Lynn are scarce. Lynn exhibited marine paintings at the British Institution between 1828 and 1838. He also exhibited at the Suffolk Street Galleries during the same period. The artist must have been well connected since many of his customers were yacht owners. He may have been an unrecorded official painter to the Royal Yacht Squadron.

Lynn was not the only artist to be inspired by Bermudian yachts. Eldon Trimingham III (b.1936), who comes from a distinguished Bermuda family, has painted many yachts in his native waters. He is especially known for his paintings of the Bermuda dinghy, a small vessel built from cedarwood which has its boom and jib projecting far out over the bow and stern. The artist's work can be found in major collections such as the Smithsonian Institution, Washington DC.

THE GOVERNMENT CUTTER *EMERALD* CRUISING IN OSBORNE BAY

Henry Sargeant (active 1830–1860s)
(oil on board, 23 x 30.5cm, dated 1831)
N R Omell Gallery.

The *Emerald* was used for general duties. Here she is flying the royal standard indicating a royal presence. It is traditionally believed that this small picture commemorates the Duchess of Kent's outing in the Solent in the summer of 1831. The duchess had leased Norris Castle for July and August of that year. Osborne House is behind the *Emerald* and Norris Castle is further to the right on the shore.

Henry Sargeant also painted the yachts that competed for the Hundred-Guinea Cup in the celebrated race of 1851. His depiction of the yacht *America* beating the Lord Anglesey's *Pearl* is now in the National Maritime Museum, Greenwich. Sargeant was almost certainly an official, although unrecorded, painter to the Royal Yacht Squadron.

ERMINIA OFF COWES CASTLE, 1880

Charles Gregory (1810–1896)
(oil on canvas, 66 x 100.5cm, circa 1880)
Royal Yacht Squadron.

This painting shows the Royal Yacht Squadron 270-ton topsail schooner *Erminia*. She was owned by Sir Bruce Chichester from 1869 to 1880 and Major William Murray from 1882 to 1884.

Charles Gregory lived in Cowes, and was therefore well placed to paint yachting subjects for club members. He exhibited only two marine paintings in London. His son George (1849–1938) was also a marine painter working chiefly on the Isle of Wight. Both artists painted yacht portraits and races often with the Royal Yacht Squadron as a backdrop. There are several fine examples of their work in the British royal collection.

A SCHOONER YACHT OFF THE NEW YORK YACHT CLUB

Archibald Cary Smith (1837–1911)
(oil on canvas, 48 x 76cm, circa 1870s)
Sotheby's, London.

The New York-born artist Archibald Cary Smith originally made his reputation designing large schooner yachts similar to those depicted in this painting. He designed many prize-winning vessels, including the defender of the 1881 America's Cup *Mischief*. She trounced the ill-prepared Canadian challenger, *Atalanta*. Not all his designs were successful, however, and *Meteor III*, a 165ft steel schooner built in 1902 for Kaiser Wilhelm II, was a poor performer.

Cary Smith, who was still working on important commissions in his early seventies had a long and successful artistic career. Between 1864 and 1869, he exhibited at the Pennsylvania Academy, and he had works shown at the National Academy of Design in New York, too. The artist also produced a number of artworks for the American magazine *Aquatic Monthly*, a short-lived publication that was established in 1872 and claimed to be 'Devoted to the interests of the Yachting and Rowing Community'. Many of Cary Smith's most popular illustrations for the magazine were later translated into engravings. The artist also taught James Gale Tyler (1855–1931), whose yachting paintings and illustrations are widely admired among enthusiasts and collectors alike.

CHAPTER IV

The Schooner Yacht America

Today the America's Cup is the most prestigious of all yacht races. It is also the longest established, with its origin in the middle of the nineteenth century. The race raised the profile of yachting to new heights, and created an international following for the sport that endures to this day.

In 1851, Britain was at the height of its imperial power and was the leading industrial nation of the day. As a showcase for British ingenuity, design and technical supremacy, Queen Victoria's consort, Prince Albert, planned the Great Exhibition in Hyde Park.

In the same year, the Earl of Wilton, Commodore of the Royal Yacht Squadron, wrote to John C Stevens, his counterpart at the New York Yacht Club, suggesting that one of the New York pilot yachts, which were renowned for their speed, should be sent to race in English waters as part of the celebrations associated with the exhibition.

John C Stevens accepted the challenge and immediately formed a syndicate to build a fast yacht. George Steers, who had a reputation for constructing the fastest pilot cutters, was chosen as the designer of the vessel, and William H Brown as its builder. Together they produced a schooner yacht of 170 tons, which was named the *America* and launched in 1851. On 22 August that year, in a race round the Isle of Wight, the *America* beat off fifteen British competitors to win the Hundred-Guinea Cup presented by the Royal Yacht Squadron.

The whole event was a humiliating experience from start to finish for the host nation. The British yachts, which included the *Beatrice*, *Volante*, *Bacchante*, *Eclipse*, *Brilliant*, *Freak*, *Alarm* and *Arrow*, came

Previous pages

◆

THE SCHOONER YACHT *AMERICA* WINNING THE HUNDRED-GUINEA CUP
(Detail)

Fitz Hugh Lane (1804–1865)
(oil on canvas, 62 x 97cm, circa 1851)
Peabody Museum, Salem, Massachusetts, United States.

This work, with some minor modifications, is a close copy of the popular lithograph by Thomas Goldsworthy Dutton after a design by Sir Oswald Walter Brierly (*see page 67*). This would explain the absence of the subtle and highly atmospheric lighting effects that are characteristic of Lane's original work. The artist produced a second image of the *America* in oils, making extensive changes to foreground and background details. The treatment of the sea and sky, and handling of light and shade are rendered with great subtlety in this far superior composition, which is now in a private collection.

In the mid-Victorian era, prints were freely available and artists thought little of copying or adapting them for their own work. In fact, this practice had been widespread in the seventeenth and eighteenth centuries. Some marine artists of the nineteenth and twentieth centuries have also been inspired by, and in some instances have directly copied or adapted, photographic sources, notably from the celebrated archive of Beken in Cowes.

nowhere near to matching the speed of *America*. *Freak* collided with *Volante*, and *Alarm*, owned by Joseph Weld, one of the most powerful figures in nineteenth-century British yachting, had to go to the assistance of *Arrow* when she ran aground.

Queen Victoria and Prince Albert had followed the proceedings from the *Victoria and Albert*, and shortly after the race they paid a visit to the winning yacht. They spent half an hour aboard the *America* and were greatly impressed. The queen gave presents to the master of the vessel, Captain Brown, and presented a commemorative gold sovereign to each crew member.

Not surprisingly, the Americans back home were quick to capitalise on their country's triumph. Printmaker Nathaniel Currier published a coloured lithograph, *The Great Exhibition of 1851*, which mocked Britain's yachting pride. The caricature included the portrayal of a bloated Englishman called Mister Bull alongside a slim and elegantly attired American colleague. One of Bull's compatriots cynically declares 'Well altho' we are beaten I am not sorry; these Americans are bone of our bone, and the origin of their genius is British'. A poem was also included on the print: 'Yankee Doodle had a craft, a rather tidy clipper, And he challenged while they laughed the Britishers to whip her, Their whole yacht squadron she outsped, and that on her own water, of all the lot she went ahead, and they came nowhere after'. To add to the Americans' delight, the United States had also done well at the Great Exhibition itself. American designers were awarded several prizes for agricultural implements, as well as for a number of other innovations, notably Colt's repeating pistol.

Following the resounding victory of the *America*, the Hundred-Guinea Cup was renamed the America's Cup in honour of the winning yacht, and was presented to the New York Yacht Club. It was then offered as a permanent challenge to yacht clubs of any nation on the understanding that the cup would be held by the winning club and not by the owner of the winning boat, a rule that still applies today.

The *America*'s success raised the standard of yacht design in general, and by the end of the nineteenth century, some of the most eminent designers had emerged: Edward Burgess, William Fife, Nathaniel Herreshoff, Charles Nicholson and George Watson. The publicity surrounding the Hundred-Guinea Cup also helped raise the profile of yachting in Britain and the United States. At the same time, successful financiers, industrialists and merchants in both countries were making vast fortunes from banking, manufacturing and trade, enabling them to enjoy luxurious cruising and to race against the crowned heads of Europe, pastimes which had previously been the preserve of a privileged few. There was also an emerging affluent middle class, which for the first time could afford to participate in small boat racing. As yacht races rapidly increased in number and popularity, the sport attracted a national and international following. This, in turn, stimulated an even greater demand for oil paintings, watercolours and prints of yachting scenes.

One of the most popular subjects was the *America* herself. John Christian Schetky, in his capacity as honorary marine painter to the Royal Yacht Squadron, would have certainly witnessed the Hundred-Guinea Cup race, and would have noticed the innovative design of the winning vessel. In his *View of Cowes with Yachts in a Calm Sea and Light Airs off Castle Point*, painted in 1852, he depicted her in the background. The picture now hangs in the Royal Yacht Squadron.

Another contemporary artist, Thomas Sewell Robins (1814–1880), painted a remarkable portrait of the *America*, also on display at the Royal Yacht Squadron (*see page 66*). The painting is dated 1852, but it was based on sketches made by on the spot. Robins collaborated with several printmakers and publishers, including Edwin Thomas Dolby (active 1840–1880) who, according to Bénézit's *Dictionnaire des peintres, sculpteurs, dessinateurs et graveurs*, was known for painting architectural views and churches.

There are also numerous portraits of the *America* by American artists. These were mainly painted after the Hundred-Guinea Cup; depictions of the yacht before her transatlantic crossing are rare. One painting of *America* by Fitz Hugh Lane (1804–1865), however, does appear to show her in American waters. It is probably a rare image of the yacht undergoing racing trials before crossing the Atlantic. The artist may well have visited New York Harbour to see the trials. Lane's painting, which is now in a private American collection, is unusual in that it shows three different views of the yacht in the same picture. L Francis Herreshoff, son of the famous American yacht designer Nathaniel Herreshoff, and a designer himself and one-time owner of the work, was adamant about the accuracy of Lane's portrayal of the vessel. In his 1963 book *An Introduction to Yachting*, he wrote: '… this painting by the accurate artist, Fitzhugh (*sic*) Lane, is very interesting. In the view from astern you can see that her sails are almost perfect airfoils, just twisted aloft correctly for the higher wind velocities there…'. As the American art historian, Erik A R Ronnberg Jr, has pointed out, although Herreshoff believed Lane's picture depicted the *America* in English waters, the inclusion of a dory in the left foreground almost certainly identifies the scene as American.

Fitz Hugh Lane was born in Gloucester, Massachusetts. Having contracted polio as a child, he was unable to move without the aid of crutches or a wheelchair, and was largely self-taught. In the early 1830s, he received some instruction from William S Pendleton, proprietor of the leading lithographic printing company in Boston. It was almost certainly here that Lane met the British marine painter Robert Salmon (1775-*c.*1844), who had settled in the city in around 1828. Salmon had a notable influence on Lane and many other American artists. He painted only a small number of yachting pictures (*see page 67*). These included a depiction of the schooner *Dream*, flagship of the Boston Boat Club, traditionally believed to be the first yacht club to be established in America. This painting is now in the Baron Thyssen-Bornemisza collection in Madrid.

Fitz Hugh Lane's portrait of *The Yacht* Northern Light *in Boston Harbour* is arguably his masterpiece in this genre (*see page 66*). The composition is far from being original, however. Lane openly acknowledged his debt to Robert Salmon by inscribing on the back of the canvas that his painting was after a sketch by the British painter. Lane's style is characterised by careful and controlled draughtsmanship, and by subjects imbued with such stillness and calm that they appear to be 'frozen in time'. Invariably, his pictures are filled with radiant light, often of remarkable luminosity. He is now acknowledged as one of America's 'blue chip' artists and 'the first native American marine painter of real stature'.

In addition to yacht portraits, Lane painted the New York Yacht Club regattas, too. These events were also painted by the collaborative New Bedford artists Albert van Beest (1820–1860) and William Bradford (1827–1892). The preparatory watercolour drawing for their oil painting of the New York Yacht Club race of 1856 was signed by both artists. It is now in the Old Dartmouth Historical Society and Whaling Museum, New Bedford, Massachusetts. Lane's pictures clearly influenced their work.

James Bard (1815–1897) is now regarded as one of the foremost American ship portraitists. According to his obituary, during the 1830s and 1840s he collaborated with his twin brother John Bard (1815–1856), but after 1849 he worked on his own. For a time, he had a studio in lower Manhattan. Bard produced portraits of several yachts, notably Commodore Voorhuis's *Tidal Wave*, which he painted in 1871. This work is now in a private collection. He also painted a portrait of the *America*, which is held in the Abbey Rockefeller Collection, Williamsburg. Bard often took representational liberties with the scale and perspective of his colourful close-up portraits of ships, steamboats and yachts. Even so, his pictures have considerable charm and are popular with contemporary collectors. Anthony Peluso Jr, a leading American maritime art historian, has been the driving force behind the current re-evaluation of the artist's work.

The increased number of yacht races in general, and especially the America's Cup, was good news for the art market and the publishing industry in the mid-nineteenth century. Artists, printmakers, printers and publishers were all keen to benefit from the sport's popularity. In particular, the new middle-class buyers, who could not afford original oil paintings, watercolour or drawings, stimulated the market for print versions and illustrated yachting periodicals. On 29 August 1851, a week after the Hundred-Guinea Cup race, the publishers S W Fores of Piccadilly in London, which described themselves as a 'Sporting & Fine Print Repository and

Frame Manufactory', placed a small advertisement on the front page of *The Times* announcing to readers that they were preparing for publication 'the schooner yacht *America*, 170 tons ... from a drawing by Mr T S Robins, forming Plate 3 of "Fores' Marine Sketches", Price 10s each coloured; 5s each plain'. Although these prints were quite expensive, they were well within the price range of an affluent middle-class customer. Those that could not afford to buy the prints, however, could either see them on display in the print shop window or else hire them for the evening for a small fee. Eager to cash in on the current taste for yachting subjects, Fores also announced their latest print venture: 'In progress, a Series of Portraits of Noted Yachts, entitled "Fores' Yachting Souvenirs"'.

Hunt's Yachting Magazine was also established as a direct result of the increased popularity of the sport following the success of the *America*. The first issue appeared in August 1852. The preface stated: 'There are at the present moment a score of Yacht Clubs in the United Kingdom, containing altogether about five thousand subscribing members.... A national sport ... ought certainly to have a Magazine, to register the regattas, cruises, crotchets, inventions, deeds, discussions, and opinions of its supporters.' The magazine lasted until the end of the nineteenth century. Many other European and American yachting magazines followed the launch of *Hunt's Yachting Magazine*, including *The Rudder*, *The Yachtsman* and *Yachting Monthly*, the latter still being published today. These magazines offered an outlet to marine artists for illustrations for yachting features and stories, as well as for covers.

One of Fores' greatest rivals in the London print trade was Ackermann & Co. Established in around 1783, this company was for many years one of London's leading print publishers, notably of colour prints. They were also a retail outlet selling a wide range of artists' materials and fancy goods. They often published maritime prints jointly with provincial publishers, notably William Foster of Portsmouth, whose name appears on many of the finest yachting prints.

Sir Oswald Walter Brierly (1817–1894) was one of Ackermann & Co's principal artists. Originally from Chester, he inherited his artistic talents from his father who was an amateur artist. After studying at Henry Sass's Drawing Academy in London, he moved to Plymouth to study naval architecture and rigging. As E H H Archibald, a well-known British maritime art historian, has pointed out, Brierly must have been one of the most travelled of professional artists. In 1841, he sailed with a friend to Rio de Janeiro, Tristan da Cunha and Sydney, Australia, in the aptly named brig-rigged yacht, *Wanderer* (*see page 70*). She was later sold in part-settlement of an unsuccessful Queensland and Antarctic whaling expedition.

In 1874, Brierly succeeded John Christian Schetky as marine painter in ordinary to Queen Victoria. As part of his official duties, he would draw the queen's yachts. He must have performed well since she bestowed a knighthood on the artist in 1885. Brierly held many other posts, too, including that of honorary marine painter to the Royal Yacht Squadron from 1875 until his death in 1894.

Brierly collaborated with the printmaker and artist Thomas Goldsworthy Dutton (*c.*1819–1891) on a number of his designs. These included a print of the victorious *America* (*see page 67*) which was published by Ackermann & Co in October 1851. This proved a very popular image: Fitz Hugh Lane adopted much of its composition in one of his own paintings of the American schooner yacht (*see page 60–1*) in the same year.

Dutton was undoubtedly the finest British maritime lithographer of his era. In 1844, he described himself as a 'Lithographic artist, marine draughtsman and draughtsman on wood…', at that time working from 146 Fleet Street in London. He excelled at ship portraits, general shipping scenes and yachting subjects. He also produced a small number of oil paintings and watercolours. As well as working for Ackermann & Co, where he lithographed more than one hundred designs, Dutton also worked for Fores and Day & Son, lithographers to Queen Victoria. He worked for various illustrated newspapers, too, including the *Illustrated London News* and *Hunt's Yachting Magazine*, for which he lithographed the designs of Arthur Wellington Fowles (1815–1883). Dutton had a good working relationship with the magazine. In the November 1852 edition, his address was published as 'Bale's Cottage, Wandsworth Rd, London' so that readers might contact him. Another snippet of information is revealed by the January 1853 edition, in which Dutton is discussed as a 'gentleman who holds the office of marine artist in the Royal Harwich and London Yacht Clubs'.

Dutton collaborated with many marine artists including Admiral Richard Brydges Beechey, William Adolphus Knell, Henry A Luscombe

(1820–*c.*1868) (*see page 70*), John Lynn, Thomas Sewell Robins, Henry Sargeant and Samuel Walters (1811–1882). Some of his best-known prints were made in collaboration with Nicholas Matthews Condy and Charles Taylor the Younger (*c.*1843–1866), who may have been Dutton's pupil. Taylor was a lithographer, and his watercolours are similar in style to those of Dutton (*see page 71*).

Dutton also collaborated with the Dublin-born artist Robert Lowe Stopford (1813–1898), who painted both marines and landscapes in watercolour. He exhibited at the Royal Hibernian Academy from 1858 to 1884 and worked for the *Illustrated London News* as their correspondent in Southern Ireland. C Rogers Senior (active 1850–1880) also produced competent coloured lithographs, although details of his life and career are speculative. He is known to have lithographed Joseph Weld's yacht *Lulworth* in 1828, and to have painted some yachting scenes in oils.

Another obscure printmaker and artist to work with Dutton on occasions was Josiah, or as he is sometimes called Joseph, Taylor (active 1850–1870). Judging from Taylor's original watercolour designs (*see pages 68–9*), he was a close rival to Dutton, and occasionally surpassed him in his careful draughtsmanship, rendering of nautical detail and clarity of design. Taylor was based in London. He worked for both Ackermann & Co and Day & Son, as well as publishing his own work.

Charles Robert Ricketts (active 1850–1880) is also worthy of mention. His yachting designs were occasionally lithographed by MacLure & Macdonald in London. He exhibited seven pictures at the Royal Academy, including *The Discovery of the North West Passage* in 1870. Ricketts also painted a number of versions of the great 1870 race across the Atlantic from Queenstown, County Cork, to New York between the schooners *Dauntless* and *Cambria*, the America's Cup challenger of that year. Ricketts portrayed *Cambria* passing Sandy Hook. Examples of Ricketts' work now hang in the Royal Thames Yacht Club, the Royal London Yacht Club, Cowes, and the New York Yacht Club. Ricketts is noteworthy because he was one of the earliest yachting artists to be influenced by photography, which had only recently been invented. His compositions were photographed and he was often inspired by the medium (*see page 71*). Several yachting painters would follow Ricketts' example, including a number of artists working today.

THE SCHOONER YACHT *AMERICA* OFF COWES, 1851

Thomas Sewell Robins (1814–1880)
(oil on canvas, 77.5 x 120.5cm, dated 1852)
Royal Yacht Squadron.

On 28 August 1851, the *America* won a private race against the English schooner *Titania*. A decade later, she was beaten at Queenstown by the Irish schooner *La Traviata* on 28 June 1861, and defeated again on 5 August by the *Alarm* in a private match at Cowes.

Today, Robins is better known as a watercolourist. He also produced oil paintings of marine and landscape subjects, however, which he exhibited at the Royal Academy between 1829 and 1874. His pictures are usually competently turned out but they invariably lack the drama and flair of fellow yachting artists, notably James Edward Buttersworth (1817–1894). But occasionally Robins' yachting scenes are of the highest rank. This portrayal of *America*, for example, is arguably his masterpiece. His restrained use of colour does not detract from the carefully drawn and atmospheric work.

THE YACHT *NORTHERN LIGHT* IN BOSTON HARBOUR

Fitz Hugh Lane
(oil on canvas, 47.5 x 66cm, dated 1845)
Shelburne Museum, Shelburne, Vermont, United States.

Northern Light was built by Whitmore Holbrook in East Boston in 1839, probably to the designs of Lewis Winde. She was one of the most successful schooner yachts before the arrival of the *America*. *Northern Light*'s design, like that of the *America*, was based on the streamlined shapes of the fast pilot schooners.

Lane's yachting pictures include a series of oil paintings of the New York Yacht Club races of the 1850s. These large-scale panoramic pictures have a low viewpoint and a matter-of-factness in their compositional arrangement, suggesting that Lane, or perhaps another artist, had witnessed the event first hand, perhaps making on-the-spot sketches and drawings from a small boat.

THE SCHOONER YACHT *AMERICA*, 1851

Thomas Goldsworthy Dutton (c.1819–1891),
after Sir Oswald Walter Brierly (1817–1894)
(tinted lithograph, 37.5 x 59.5cm, published by
Ackermann & Co, 22 October 1851)
Royal Thames Yacht Club.

Sir Oswald Walter Brierly had a talent for producing marine watercolours that were suitable for translation into prints. Ackermann's published many of his drawings and watercolours, often lithographed by Thomas Goldsworthy Dutton and printed by Day & Haghe. Coloured versions of the sepia print shown here were also produced.

Thomas Goldsworthy Dutton is now widely regarded as the most gifted, and one of the most prolific, lithographers of his generation. He was also a skilful watercolourist and would sometimes make a lithograph from his own preparatory design. Dutton prints were very expensive. In the 1860s, they sold for around £1 10s, at a time when the average weekly wage was about the same. By collaborating with other publishers the production costs of the venture could be shared.

A CUTTER YACHT OF THE NORTHERN YACHT CLUB, NEAR DUNOON

Robert Salmon (1775–c.1845)
(oil on panel, 51 x 78cm, circa 1830)
Vallejo Maritime Gallery.

From 1825 to 1830, the sport of yachting dramatically increased in popularity in Britain. In 1824, the Northern Yacht Club of Great Britain (later the Royal Northern Yacht Club) was established in Belfast. Six years later, the club received the prefix 'Royal', and moved to Scotland. Towards the end of the nineteenth century, some of the greatest yacht designers were based in the country, most notably William Fife and George Watson on the River Clyde.

This picture by Robert Salmon shows a cutter yacht flying the club's burgee as she cruises off Clark Light near the town of Dunoon on the Clyde. Salmon is better known for his ship portraits and harbour and coastal scenes. His portraits of yachts are comparatively rare.

GLORIANA WINNING A RACE AGAINST *XANTHA*, 15 JUNE 1869
(*Detail*)

Josiah Taylor (active 1850–1870)
(watercolour on paper, 39 x 67cm, circa 1869)
Royal Thames Yacht Club.

The *Gloriana* was built in 1852 by Ratsey of Cowes. She was supposed to resemble the *America*. She won many notable races, including the Prince Consort's Cup in 1852 and the Nore-to-Cherbourg race in 1868. The Prince of Wales's steam yacht *Alexandra*, in the right foreground wearing the prince's commodore's pendant, acted as the committee vessel during the race.

This watercolour was published as a lithograph on 30 June 1870, by Ackermann & Co. Next to nothing is known about the printmaker and artist Josiah Taylor. It is clear from this painting, however, that he was a skilled draughtsman with a keen eye for nautical detail.

THE YACHT *WANDERER* OF THE ROYAL YACHT SQUADRON

Sir Oswald Walters Brierly
(watercolour with gouache, 44.5 x 25cm, dated 1842)
Royal Thames Yacht Club.

In 1841, Brierly set sail for Sydney, by way of Tenerife, Tristan da Cunha and Rio de Janeiro, in the yacht *Wanderer*, accompanied by his friend, Benjamin Boyd, a London stockbroker. In this atmospheric watercolour, which Brierly made on the voyage, the *Wanderer* is depicted arriving off Inaccessible Island, near Tristan da Cunha, in the South Atlantic Ocean. The yacht's crew are shooting at sea birds. In 1850, Boyd set off on another shooting expedition to the Solomon Islands, but he disappeared without trace.

For a time, Brierly settled in New Zealand and made a number of useful naval contacts, enabling him to travel on board Royal Navy vessels. In 1850, he was cruising aboard HMS *Meander* in the Pacific and off the west coast of South America with the ship's captain, the Honourable Harry Keppel. During the cruise, Brierly made sketches, drawings and watercolours, which he later translated into coloured lithographs. He rarely worked in oils.

A REGATTA AT PLYMOUTH

Henry Andrews Luscombe (1820–c.1868)
(oil on board, 23 x 35.5cm, circa 1850)
N R Omell Gallery.

This small oil painting depicts an unidentified yachting regatta of the early 1850s, possibly off the southwest coast of England. Luscombe is a little-known artist who had a successful studio in Plymouth. He exhibited at the Royal Academy between 1845 and 1865. He also collaborated with the maritime lithographer Thomas Goldsworthy Dutton. Examples of Luscombe's work can be found in the Plymouth Art Gallery, Plymouth, England, and the National Maritime Museum, Greenwich.

CUTTERS RACING OFF THE ROYAL YACHT SQUADRON'S HEADQUARTERS

Charles Robert Ricketts (active 1850–1880)
(oil on canvas, 45.8 x 76.2cm, circa 1860)
Bonhams Auctioneers, London.

Marine artists frequently used the Royal Yacht Squadron at Cowes as a backdrop for their yachting subjects, and Ricketts was no exception. Although the artist made many versions of his most successful works, his pictures rarely come on to the market. This painting, however, was one of a pair sold by Bonhams in 1996. Ricketts was often inspired by photographic sources, and in turn his work was sometimes photographed itself. His painting showing the 1870 Atlantic yacht race, *Cambria passing Sandy Hook*, for example, appeared as a sepia photograph laid on card. A copy of the photograph, acknowledged to the photographers Brown & Wheeler of Cowes, is now part of the New York Yacht Club's library collection. A version of Ricketts' painting hangs in the Royal Thames Yacht Club in London.

THE CUTTER *FIONA*

Thomas Goldsworthy Dutton
(watercolour and bodycolour,
35 x 66.5cm, circa 1867)
Royal Thames Yacht Club.

The elegantly shaped *Fiona*, designed by William Fife, is shown here winning the Royal Western of Ireland's Queen's Cup on 20 July 1867 at Queenstown. She was owned by Mr E Boucher of the Royal Thames Yacht Club. Original watercolour designs and lithographs by Dutton are highly sought after by collectors. He occasionally painted in oils.

CHAPTER V

Nineteenth-Century Yachting:
Deck Scenes and Races

REPRESENTATIONS OF YACHT DECK SCENES AND CREWS ARE RARE IN YACHTING ART. PERHAPS THIS IS BECAUSE WEALTHY YACHT OWNERS DID NOT WANT PICTURES THAT SHOWED THE WORKING ASPECT OF THE SPORT, BUT PREFERRED INSTEAD WORKS THAT EMPHASISED THE COMFORT, ELEGANCE AND GRACE OF THEIR CHOSEN PASTIME. OR PERHAPS IT IS SIMPLY BECAUSE YACHTING ARTISTS WERE MORE ADEPT AT PAINTING VESSELS THAN FIGURES.

Nicholas Matthews Condy's deck scene aboard the cutter *Alarm*, however, is both a masterpiece of yachting art and a fine example of portraiture (*see pages 72-3*). As well as offering an authentic view of the appearance of a yacht at close quarters, albeit with some economy or embellishment befitting a great artist, the painting also realistically shows the arrangement of the yacht's gear, and the personalities associated with the sport.

Nicholas Matthews Condy (1818–1851) died at the young age of thirty-three. But in his short life he painted all manner of yachting subjects and raised the standard of yachting art to new heights. Condy was born in Union Street, Plymouth, southwest England, and was educated at Mount Radford School in nearby Exeter. He abandoned a career in the army to take up marine painting. He was taught by his father, also called Nicholas Condy (1799–1857), who occasionally painted marine subjects but preferred seashore scenes with fisherfolk and cottage interiors with carefully drawn figures. Their work is often confused.

Nicholas Matthews Condy was a precocious talent. It is traditionally believed that the Earl of Egremont, a patron of J M W Turner, once visited his home, and after seeing a sketch of the yacht *Kestrel*, immediately paid ten guineas for it. Condy was only thirteen at the time. No doubt encouraged by this early experience and by his father's tuition, Condy went on to become one of the most popular artists of his time and one of the most accomplished of all British yachting artists. His remarkable deck scenes, portraying yacht owners and their families, yachtsmen and crew, have never been surpassed. As well as his close-up view of the *Alarm*, two other similar works by Condy are known: one shows the yacht *Guerrilla* (*see page 79*) with Captain Ward and his family on board, and the other portrays the *Gondola* with her crew. Both are small-scale panel pictures.

Condy also painted the famous 1843 race on the River Thames between Lord Alfred Paget's *Mystery* and A Fountaine's *Blue Bell* (*see page 80*), during which the *Blue Bell* ran aground, allowing *Mystery* to win. Condy's oil painting of *The Royal Thames Regatta at the Nore, 1844* (*see page 80*) is a yachting masterpiece. It combines nautical accuracy with a carefully balanced and harmonious composition and convincing naturalistic effects. Both paintings now hang in the Royal Thames Yacht Club.

In his lifetime, Condy became the official marine painter to both the Royal Thames Yacht Club and the Royal Western Yacht Club, based in Plymouth. He also exhibited three times at the Royal Academy. In 1842 and 1845, he chose to submit naval subjects, and for his 1844 exhibit he produced the portrait *The Royal Steam Yacht* Victoria and Albert *entering Plymouth Sound, 30 August 1843*. Condy also painted Tsar Nicholas I of Russia's schooner yacht *Queen Victoria*. Built by Joseph White of Cowes, under the supervision of Lord Mount Edgecumbe, a patron of the Condy family, the *Queen*

Previous pages
◆
WILLIAM JOHN FORSTER ON BOARD THE YACHT *ALARM*
(*Detail*)

Nicholas Matthews Condy (1818-1851)
(oil on panel, 33 x 45.5cm, circa 1840)
National Maritime Museum, Greenwich.

The yacht *Alarm* is seen in Plymouth Sound with the Mew Stone visible on the port bow. Some of the crew are preparing to cast off the mooring; one crew member is waiting to hoist a signal flag and a steward carries a plate of ham towards the saloon companionway. The yacht's owner, Joseph Weld, a founder member of the Royal Yacht Squadron, is seated centre right wearing a tall hat. The ornate frame of this picture is inscribed 'Royal Yacht Squadron' suggesting the picture was a special commission for a member of the club, perhaps Joseph Weld himself, who was an influential figure in the sport and owner of several prominent yachts, including the *Charlotte*, *Arrow* and *Lulworth*. The young man on the left with outstretched arms is traditionally identified as the yachtsman, William John Forster.

The *Alarm* was built in 1830 for Joseph Weld. Of 193 tons, she was one of largest yachts ever launched. She was designed to beat the largest and most outstanding yachts of the period and won the King William IV Cup in 1838 and the Queen's Cup on four separate occasions between 1844 and 1861.

Victoria was launched in 1846 and was at the time the most modern yacht afloat. In 1847, members of the Royal Yacht Squadron sailed their yachts to St Petersburg to compete for and win a gold cup presented by the tsar.

Condy's yachting paintings, sketches and drawings were often reproduced in illustrated weekly newspapers. These publications were responding to the growing popular demand for illustrations and stories on yachts and races. Many of Condy's designs were translated into prints by Thomas Goldsworthy Dutton and published by Fores of Piccadilly. Fores also employed Thomas Picken (active 1846–1875) to lithograph Condy's work. In addition to yachts, Condy painted naval subjects and harbour and coastal scenes, often with his native Plymouth as a backdrop. Between 1845 and 1850, the period when he was producing acclaimed work for members of the Royal Thames Yacht Club, Condy was also providing naval illustrations to one of the leading British illustrated periodicals, the *Illustrated London News*. In later life, he became a painting teacher in his native city, where he was buried after his death in 1851.

Condy's wife, Flora Ross Condy, shared her husband's passion for yachting and cruising. In particular, she enjoyed sailing at Cowes, which by the mid-nineteenth century had became the social centre for yachting. In 1843, Flora wrote of the week in August when the monarch attended the Isle of Wight, popularly known as 'Cowes Week': 'A week at Cowes is pleasant enough, provided it is the Regatta Week, and you have a sail every day, and do everything that is to be done in the way of gaiety; so we got on very well, between sails round the Island, champagne luncheons, a very pleasant archery meeting at Carisbrooke, and a final wind up with the Royal Yacht Squadron Ball, usually gay, and certainly the most amusing one at which I ever had the good fortune to be present.'

Flora Condy also had first-hand experience of yachting and in 1843 she went for a cruise aboard J H W Smyth-Pigott's 70ft yacht *Ganymede*. The cruise began at Cowes and ended at Plymouth. In a book she wrote after her husband's death, Flora described the battle against rough weather during the trip. The book, which was called simply *Reminiscences of a Yachting Cruise* and was dedicated to Condy's memory, was published by Ackermann & Co in 1852 with four tinted lithographic prints by Dutton after the artist's sketches. These included portraits of the yachts *Xarifa* and *Kestrel*.

Condy was not alone in portraying the *Alarm*. The Victorian artist Joseph Miles Gilbert also depicted the yacht, although in a more traditional way. Gilbert showed her winning the Ladies' Cheltenham Challenge Cup at Cowes in 1830, the year of her launch (*see page 78*). For most of his life, Gilbert lived in Lymington in Hampshire, England. He trained to be an painter, and exhibited twice at the Royal Academy, in 1825 and 1855. It seems that his contemporaries placed him in high regard. The Royal Academy awarded him one gold and one silver medal for his marine paintings, and he was appointed official marine painter to the Royal Solent Yacht Club, of which he was also a member. In 1832, several lithographs of Gilbert's paintings were published in the book *Views of the Principal Seats and Marine Landscape Scenery in the Neighbourhood of Lymington, drawn on stone by Louis Haghe from original paintings done on the spot by J M Gilbert*. These prints included the portrait of the *Alarm*. According to Timothy P McDonnell, a direct descendant of Gilbert, the artist was fastidious over his art and would '... tear work up he did not like, one reason why his work is so rare.' McDonnell also believes that Louis Haghe, one of Queen Victoria's official lithographers, introduced Gilbert to the queen and a friendship developed between her and the artist.

James Edward Buttersworth (1817–1894) is regarded by many American maritime collectors today as the doyen of nineteenth-century yachting artists. He painted many marine subjects, notably packet ships, clippers, steamers and some naval actions, but he was especially fond of yachts. His yachting scenes were painted, often on a small scale, with a vigour and passion that rank them among the finest ever produced. The artist's popularity lies in his ability to create harmonious compositions, combined with his skilful handling of light and use of atmospheric effects. More importantly for his customers, who were often yachtsmen, his vessels were painted with a high degree of accuracy. John Wilmerding, in his *American Marine Painting*, rightly asserts that Buttersworth's 'understanding of rigging and the setting of the sails under way was unrivalled, and he matched his understanding with careful drawing.'

Genealogical records suggest that Buttersworth's father was the English marine painter Thomas Buttersworth (1768–1842). Thomas had served in the British Royal Navy and he is best remembered today for his naval actions and general shipping scenes. He probably gave his son his first artistic instruction. Although English by birth, James rightly belongs to the American school since his mature work was painted in the United States. He emigrated to the country with his family in the 1840s, settling initially in Manhattan, New York, and later moving to West Hoboken, New Jersey. He was a private man whose interests centred on his family and his art.

Buttersworth painted a wide range of yachting subjects, including yacht portraits, famous races and the New York Yacht Club's regattas. Although he did not attempt to paint close-up deck scenes or portraits of yachtsmen and their families, as Condy had done, Buttersworth was very concerned with capturing nautical detail in his portraits of yachts, and he occasionally showed the crew working the vessels (*see page 81*). The artist's favourite subjects were the schooner yacht *America* and the other boats that competed in the America's Cup races. As Richard Grassby has noted, Buttersworth 'lived long enough to record eight challengers and numerous trials, and the America's Cup may be said to have presented him with his greatest challenge as a marine artist'.

The Sloop Maria *racing the Schooner Yacht* America, *May 1851* (*see page 84*) is not only one of Buttersworth's finest yachting paintings, but is also unquestionably the most important painting of *America* undergoing sea trials before she crossed the Atlantic to compete in the Hundred-Guinea Cup. The *America*'s builder, William H Brown, had promised that he would build a yacht 'faster than any vessel in the United States brought to compete against her' on penalty of her being returned with no payment if she should fail such a trial. Despite Brown's claims, however, the *America* performed badly against the *Maria*. Even so, the race syndicate organised by John C Stevens still decided to bring *America* to England to compete, although it shrewdly negotiated a reduction in her purchase price from $30,000 to $20,000. It is now believed that Buttersworth was in England to witness the Hundred-Guinea Cup. The existence of several paintings by the artist showing British subjects at the time of the famous Isle of Wight race reinforces this supposition.

Of Buttersworth's many other depictions of the America's Cup challenges, his oil painting of the *Mayflower* leading the *Galatea* in the 1886 race ranks as one of his masterpieces (*see page 85*). It shows the contest between Lieutenant William Henn of the Royal Navy and Charles J Paine of the US Army. Henn's *Galatea* was defeated 2–0.

Many of Buttersworth's pictures were made into prints and published in the United States. In the mid-nineteenth century, the leading lithographic publishing firms in America were William & John Pendleton's of Boston, Nathaniel Currier, later Currier & Ives, based in New York, and Endicott & Co. Buttersworth is known to have collaborated with two of Currier's in-house lithographers, Frances Flora Palmer (*c.*1820–1876), known as Fanny, and Charles Parsons (1821–1910), both of whom were originally from England, but had emigrated to America. As well as being largely responsible for translating Buttersworth's designs of clipper ships, yachts and regattas into lithographs, they were also gifted artists in their own right. From 1863, Parsons worked for the Harpers, who published *Harper's Magazine* and *Harper's Weekly*, assisting in the design and production of wood engravings for illustrations. He also excelled as a yachting artist, and painted a number of yacht portraits and regattas (*see page 81*).

One of the most popular lithographs to be published in the United States by Nathaniel Currier was Fanny Palmer's 1852 print of Buttersworth's painting showing the race between the *Maria* and the *America*. In the original picture, Buttersworth had changed the angle of the trailing *America* to display the full broadside of the vessel. But in her version, Palmer altered this artistic indulgence, turning the *America* 180 degrees.

The popularity of Palmer's lithograph in the United States may have been matched in Britain. It certainly appears that the print was known by British artists. As part of Fores' series of marine sketches, Thomas Sewell Robins produced a preparatory design of the *Maria*. The American yacht never visited England, however, so Robins could not have drawn her first hand. Instead, he seems to have based his design on Palmer's print. Robins' broadside view of the *Maria*, lithographed by Thomas Goldsworthy Dutton and published by Fores in June 1853, is very similar in appearance to Buttersworth's image of the yacht.

Buttersworth also painted transatlantic crossings, notably the Great Transatlantic Race of 1866, the first fully crewed yacht race across the Atlantic. The contest had come about after the tobacco magnate Pierre Lorillard had bragged at a New York dinner party in October 1866 that his schooner yacht *Vesta* was the fastest vessel afloat. His claim was disputed by the newspaper tycoon James Gordon Bennett Jr, who owned *Henrietta*, and George and Franklin Osgood, owners of *Fleetwing*. To settle the dispute, the yacht owners planned a race from Sandy Hook, New York, to the Needles off the Isle of Wight, with the winner earning the incredible sum of $90,000. Starting on 11 December 1866, the race was won by Bennett's *Henrietta*, which arrived at the Needles on Christmas Day, completing the course in a time of thirteen days, twenty-one hours and four minutes.

Bennett almost certainly commissioned the American artist Julius L Stewart (1855–1919) to commemorate his triumph (*see page 82*). Stewart's oval painting can be seen today as a centrepiece of a specially carved elaborate stone fireplace in the model room of the New York Yacht Club. Stewart also painted Bennett with his friends aboard his 226ft yacht *Namouna* in 1890. The famous actress Lily Langtry was one of the guests. The yacht's interior features included Louis Tiffany glass decoration, a dining hall, offices and nine staterooms.

Although Buttersworth's picture of the race, painted in around 1870, is a small-scale work, it has great subtlety and charm, and is an important record of an historic event. The sophistication of Buttersworth's art is evident if his watercolour of the schooner yacht *Dauntless* (*see page 82*) is compared with that of the *Glimpse* (*see page 83*), painted by the Boston-based artist Joseph W Pierce (active 1865–1889). Pierce's naive painting style allies him with the so-called Pier Head painters. This is a blanket term which covers the many self-taught artists all over the world who tried to secure commissions from visiting ships. Often they had first-hand maritime experience. They would work hard to complete a picture in time for the ship to sail or else they would lose their fee. They were first and foremost ship portraitists and if they were capable of rendering a vessel with an acceptable degree of accuracy they could make a living. Sea and landscape details, and the inclusion of figures, were often regarded as less important since the main focus was on the ship, and as such the treatment of these features is usually less convincing.

Haughton Forrest (1826–1925) is a little-known artist today, but he often came close to rivalling Buttersworth as a superlative yachting painter. Unfortunately, however, his work in this area is rare. The primary source of information on the artist is George Deas Brown's book, *Haughton Forrest,*

published in 1982. Forrest was born at Boulogne-sur-Mer in France. As a child, he travelled extensively with his family. He later returned to England and obtained a five-year commission in the Honourable Artillery Company, before turning to painting. He painted a number of maritime subjects, although his yacht portraits and regatta scenes are generally considered his finest works (*see page 86*).

In 1876, Forrest and his wife emigrated to Australia, settling in Tasmania. Almost immediately, he began exhibiting British coastal subjects. At that time, there was a growing interest in yachting in Australia. In the introduction to his *Reminiscences of Twenty-Five Years Yachting in Australia – An Essay on Manly Sports, A Cruise on Shore & c*, published in 1888, W H Bundy, Commodore of the South Australian Yacht Club, forcefully reminded the English that their 'Australian cousins have no more forgotten the fine old pastime [yachting] than they have cricket and rowing'.

Forrest's early work was characterised by great detail and a vigorous painterly style. From the 1880s, the influence of photography became apparent in some of his paintings. After arriving in Tasmania, he had befriended the Scotsman James Watt Beattie, who worked with Anson Brothers, a Hobart photographic firm. Beattie travelled around Australia and the Pacific, and would bring back photographs which Forrest would use as the basis for his paintings. Although the artist still produced highly detailed pictures at this time, there was little evidence of his earlier bold brushwork. Instead, his compositions became rather matter-of-fact and his technique controlled. It is as if he were painting through the lens of the camera.

Forrest was an influential marine artist in his adopted country. The Australian artist Herbert B Rollings (active 1880–1920), for example, is likely to have been one of his pupils. He produced views of yachting subjects in a highly unusual and personal manner (*see page 87*). Forrest was also almost certainly familiar with Isaac Walter Jenner (1836–1902), another British artist who emigrated to Australia. As a youth, Jenner went to sea in oyster and crab smacks. He later joined the Royal Navy and served throughout the Crimean War. After leaving the navy, he settled in Brighton and became a professional marine painter, specialising in yachting scenes off the south coast of England (*see pages 88–9*). He continued to paint English subjects even after leaving for Australia in 1883.

THE YACHT *ALARM*

Joseph Miles Gilbert (1799–1876)
(oil on canvas, 66 x 89.5cm, dated 1830)
National Maritime Museum, Greenwich.

In 1827, the lady members of the Royal Yacht Club at Cowes presented a cup of the value of 250 guineas to be sailed for by yachts of any tonnage belonging to the club. The competition, the Ladies' Cheltenham Challenge Cup, was to be open to challenge annually until awarded to some one member in three successive seasons. Whoever won the cup three times in a row would be allowed to keep the prize permanently, and would earn the title Champion of the Club. The *Alarm* is shown here winning the cup in 1830, thereby making her owner Joseph Weld, who had also won the prize in 1828 and 1829, the Champion of the Club. More than twenty years later, in 1852, the year after the Hundred-Guinea Cup was first contested, the yacht's bow form and rig was altered to resemble those of the winner, *America*. At the same time, her tonnage was increased from 193 to 248 tons. These changes greatly improved *Alarm*'s performance, and in 1860 she defeated *America* herself, although the latter, then under English ownership, had also been much changed. Louis Haghe translated this painting into a popular lithograph.

THE YACHT *GUERRILLA*

Nicholas Matthews Condy
(oil on panel, 35.5 x 45.7cm, circa 1840)
Private Collection.

Of 35 tons, *Guerrilla* (or *Guerilla*) was owned by Captain Charles Ward, who was on the list of the Royal Yacht Squadron from 1827 to 1833. The yacht's port of registry was Southampton.

This work, one of Condy's finest, is unusual in that it is a commemorative portrait showing a yacht owner with his family aboard his vessel, a very rare subject for yachting artists. It is full of charm and delightful detail. The name of the yacht appears on the stern of its tender, while a crewman hoists a signal flag in the background. Captain Ward himself is shown holding a telescope. The figure group of Ward's wife and his two daughters is painted with uncompromising care, revealing the weary expressions on the girls' faces. The artificial lighting and carefully planned composition of the work suggest that Condy executed it in his studio rather than on the spot. The family may well have visited Condy's studio for several sittings. The figures compare favourably with those painted by Condy's father, Nicholas Condy. It is likely that the two artists collaborated on this work.

THE ROYAL THAMES REGATTA AT THE NORE, 1844

Nicholas Matthews Condy
(oil on canvas, 44.5 x 59cm, dated 1844)
Royal Thames Yacht Club.

Yachts of the Royal Thames Yacht Club, which is now located in Knightsbridge, London, are seen here racing from Greenwich to the Nore and back. Six 25-ton yachts took part. This event was regarded as a trial for a cup race of 1844, offered by the Royal Yacht Squadron to yachts of any royal club of no more than 25 tons.

Condy originally presented this painting to the winner of the regatta. He has adopted a low viewpoint to create the impression that the viewer is in the midst of the action. In fact, he may well have witnessed the event. The artist had a natural ability to create accurate and striking compositions to please both yachtsmen and art lovers. His painting style is characterised by fluid brushwork and a creamy palette highlighted by an economical use of brilliant colour.

BLUE BELL AND MYSTERY

Nicholas Matthews Condy
(oil on canvas, 30 x 39.5cm, circa 1843)
Royal Thames Yacht Club.

The spectators on the bank near False Point applaud General Lord Alfred Paget's iron cutter *Mystery*, the vessel closest to the shore, as she sails on to win the Thames race in 1843. Alongside *Mystery* can be seen Mr A Fountaine's *Blue Bell* which has run aground. Lord Paget was Clerk Marshall to Queen Victoria, and between 1846 and 1873 was Commodore of the Royal Thames Yacht Club.

A preparatory watercolour design for this painting is now in a private collection. Condy's design was later lithographed by Thomas Goldsworthy Dutton.

THE NEW YORK YACHT CLUB REGATTA: THE START FROM THE STAKE BOAT IN THE NARROWS

Currier & Ives, after Charles Parsons and Attwater
(Hand-coloured lithograph, 64.5 x 81cm,
published 1869)
New York Yacht Club.

This lithograph print depicts the start of the New York Yacht Club's annual regatta from the grounds of the club's station at Stapleton on Staten Island. Among the schooners portrayed are *Vesta, Henrietta* and *Fleetwing,* the three competitors in the great transatlantic race of 1866. The number and variety of spectators crowding the shore, some dressed in top hats and fine frocks, others in less elegant, everyday outfits, give some indication of the growing popularity and the near-universal appeal of yachting regattas in the United States during the mid-nineteenth century.

THE SCHOONER *RESOLUTE* LEADING THE FLEET AROUND CASTLE GARDEN, NEW YORK

James Edward Buttersworth (1817–1894)
(oil on canvas, 56 x 92cm, circa 1870s)
Private Collection.

A S Hatch's schooner-rigged yacht *Resolute* dominates this panoramic composition. Of 200 tons, she measured 114ft in length, with a beam of 25ft 1in and a draught of 9ft 2in.

In seventeenth-century Dutch marine painting, often more than two-thirds of the picture space would be sky. Buttersworth has followed the tradition in this painting, one of his finest works. The light pink tones of the sky contrast with the strip of green sea. The artist has skilfully conveyed the effects of wind acting against sails and the fluttering of the flags ashore. Buttersworth also pays great attention to nautical detail and portrays the crew of *Resolute* actually working the vessel.

THE GREAT TRANSATLANTIC YACHT RACE, 1866

Julius L Stewart (1855–1919)
(oil on canvas, diameter 287cm, circa 1880)
New York Yacht Club.

This oval painting, which hangs above the magnificent fireplace in the model room of the New York Yacht Club, was probably commissioned by James Gordon Bennett Jr, the owner of the winning yacht, *Henrietta*.

Stewart was born in Philadelphia and is better known for landscape and genre pictures. He studied in Paris and exhibited in Europe and America, winning many prizes. His contemporary E C Peterson also painted the 1866 race. His painting, now hanging in the reception of the New York Yacht Club, is a masterly work, by an artist who deserves more recognition. Peterson exhibited at the National Academy of Design in New York.

THE SCHOONER YACHT *DAUNTLESS*

James Edward Buttersworth
(watercolour on paper, 22.8 x 33cm, circa 1869)
Vallejo Maritime Gallery.

In 1867, the *Dauntless*, owned by Commodore James Gordon Bennett, sailed across the Atlantic to race in British waters. Three years later, in 1870, she raced Sir James Ashbury's schooner the *Cambria*, the America's Cup challenger of that year, back across the Atlantic. She was narrowly beaten.

Buttersworth painted the *Dauntless* many times. Composed of light washes, with careful delineation of the sails and rigging, this delicate watercolour is a rare example of the artist's work in this medium. Buttersworth painted almost exclusively in oils. Today his watercolours rarely come onto the market.

THE SCHOONER YACHT *GLIMPSE*

Joseph W Pierce (active 1865–1889)
(watercolour on paper, 61 x 94cm, dated 1869)
Vallejo Maritime Gallery.

This unusual watercolour portrays the 56ft schooner yacht *Glimpse* in two positions as she sails in the waters off Salem, Massachusetts. Baker's Island lighthouse can be seen in the right background. The *Glimpse* was owned by a member of the Boston Yacht Club.

Little is known of the artist Joseph W Pierce except that he worked in both watercolours and oils between the 1860s and 1880s, and that he almost certainly had first-hand sailing experience. In comparison to Buttersworth's realistic and sophisticated rendering of *Dauntless* sailing across an undulating swell (*opposite*), Pierce's large work appears laboured and formulaic, although atmospheric and full of charm.

THE SLOOP *MARIA* RACING THE SCHOONER YACHT *AMERICA*, MAY 1851

James Edward Buttersworth
(oil on canvas, 38 x 61cm, circa 1851)
Private Collection.

This oil painting shows the celebrated yacht *America* just after she was launched. She is seen here undergoing racing trials against the *Maria*, which had the upper hand and brought into question the future of *America* racing in English waters. *Maria* was originally built to the designs of Robert L Stevens as a New York sloop at Hoboken in 1845. She was said to have cost $100,000 and was altered many times.

Buttersworth was normally careful to produce paintings which accurately portrayed the sport of yachting. Here, however, he has changed the angle at which the trailing *America* was sailing to display the full broad side of the vessel. His artistic indulgence was altered by Fanny Palmer in her lithograph, which was published by Nathaniel Currier in 1852. Palmer turned *America* around, so that she was racing in the same direction as *Maria*. She also altered other details.

MAYFLOWER LEADING GALATEA

James Edward Buttersworth
(oil on canvas, 65 x 77.5m, circa 1886)
Private Collection.

Buttersworth has depicted here the first of the two races that made up the sixth America's Cup challenge, which took place on 7 September 1886. The defender and eventual winner of the cup, the sloop *Mayflower*, was designed by Edward Burgess and built in 1886 by George Lawley & Son for General Charles J Paine. The challenger, *Galatea*, was designed in 1885 by J Beavor-Webb for Lieutenant William Henn RN.

In this picture, the rain-filled cumulus clouds form a contrasting backdrop to the brilliantly lit sails of the *Mayflower*, which overshadows *Galatea* in second place. This was a convention derived from the Dutch tradition of marine painting. Buttersworth invariably paid great attention to his skies, and was well aware that they offered the ideal counterpoint to the rhythmic pattern of the waves and the curving shape of a yacht's sails.

THE YACHT *ARROW* OF THE ROYAL YACHT SQUADRON

Haughton Forrest (1826–1925)
(oil on canvas, 41 x 69cm, circa *1851)*
Sotheby's, London.

Thomas Chamberlayne's ill-fated yacht *Arrow* ran aground during the famous Hundred-Guinea Cup Race around the Isle of Wight in 1851. One of Joseph Weld's yachts, *Alarm*, went to her assistance. As well as producing portraits of celebrated sailing yachts, Forrest also painted steam vessels. His paintings of great races and regattas are generally regarded as his most accomplished works.

THE CUTTER *MOONVISION* RACING OFF TASMANIA

Herbert B Rollings (active 1880–1920)
(oil on board, 25.5 x 46cm, circa 1880)
N R Omell Gallery.

This dramatic and unusual view moves away from the traditional portrait of a racing yacht. It shows the cutter *Moonvision* at close quarters, heeled over on the port tack, probably sailing in waters off Hobart, Tasmania. Racing was taking place in Tasmania as early as 1831, and in 1838 the Royal Hobart Regatta Association was established. Rollings was an Australian artist whose earthy palette and painting style are reminiscent of the work of Haughton Forrest, with whom he would almost certainly have been acquainted. He may have been his pupil. Here Rollings has not only captured the warm, glowing colours of late afternoon, but also the excitement and danger of ocean racing.

The Scottish-born painter Bill Mearns (b.1951) has lived and worked in Tasmania for the past twenty years. He has painted a number of yachting subjects, including the Sydney-to-Hobart race, which was first contested in 1945 and is now one of Australia's most important ocean races. Mearns uses a friend's fishing boat as a floating studio, and he also makes models of yachts to help his work.

AMERICAN RACING YACHTS OFF COWES, ISLE OF WIGHT

(Detail)

Isaac Walter Jenner (1836-1902)
(oil on board, 23 x 61cm, dated July 1867)
N R Omell Gallery.

Even in this small-scale, panoramic picture, the English-born artist Jenner has created a forceful composition. He has skilfully depicted the movement of the yachts through the water and the wind in the sails, and he has enlivened the scene with a liberal inclusion of seagulls.

After emigrating to Australia in 1883, Jenner became a founder member of the Queensland Art Society, an organisation formed as a result of his petitions to the Queensland government for a public art gallery. Examples of his work can be found in the Queensland Art Gallery and in the Brighton Art Gallery in England.

CHAPTER VI

Nineteenth-Century Yacht Portraits

During the nineteenth century, as more and more people in Britain and the United States bought their own yachts and discovered the joys of racing and cruising, the market for yacht portraits rapidly grew. And as owners looked towards new yacht designs and means of propulsion, artists adapted their work to reflect and cater for the changing tastes.

One of the most popular British yacht portraitists of the nineteenth century was Arthur Wellington Fowles (1815–1883). He was a prolific artist, who deserves to be better known. Fowles was born at Ryde on the Isle of Wight, where he remained for most of his life. Thus, he is widely referred to as Arthur Wellington Fowles of Ryde. He was never far away from the sea or from yachts, and he painted many pictures of the Isle of Wight, in particular subjects associated with Queen Victoria's visits to her official residence on the island, Osborne House. Fowles often painted his yacht portraits in pairs and sets. He also portrayed yacht races, royal occasions and naval vessels. Some of his designs were translated into wood engravings for the *Illustrated London News*. Although many of Fowles's paintings are of uneven quality, at its best his work is highly accomplished and noteworthy. In any case, it is clear that he was a popular artist in his own day. Just as his contemporary in America, James Edward Buttersworth, received commissions from members of the New York Yacht Club, so too Fowles painted many yacht portraits for Royal Yacht Squadron members (*see page 95*). He also painted yachts of the Royal Dart Yacht Club, which was founded in 1866 and granted a royal charter six years later.

George Crowninshield of Salem, Massachusetts, owned two of the most famous early American yachts. He used his first vessel, the 22-ton sloop *Jefferson*, built in 1801, for cruising and as a training ship. In 1816, he replaced *Jefferson* with the lavish *Cleopatra's Barge* of 191 tons at a reputed cost of $50,000. Crowninshield was more inclined to cruising than racing, and in the summer of 1817, he set off in *Cleopatra's Barge* to tour the Mediterranean. Both of Crowninshield's yachts caused a great deal of excitement wherever they sailed, and they were always popular subjects for Pier Head artists, especially those working in Italy.

Throughout the nineteenth century there were many competent Mediterranean artists working in both gouache, an opaque form of watercolour, and oils. Like Fowles, they would occasionally paint pairs of yacht portraits, often featuring the vessel in fair and foul weather conditions.

Although most of these ship and yacht portraitists were anonymous, and remain so to this day, some were named. Among them were L Papaluca and Tomaso (active 1850–1900) and Antonio (active 1860–1920) de Simone, all of whom painted in Naples. It is not known with any degree of certainty whether the de Simones were actually related, although it is generally believed that they were father and son. They cashed in on the constant requests from the many European and American yacht owners cruising the Mediterranean, who desired portraits of their vessels as souvenirs of their trip. The artists had to paint quickly before the owners sailed on to their next port of call. This meant their works often lack the precise nautical detail normally demanded by yachtsmen. However, their customers appreciated the charming atmospheric effects of their paintings, which also frequently included a smoking Mount Vesuvius as a romantic and nostalgic backdrop. The de Simones were very popular artists and few private yachts escaped their attention. They also painted Royal Navy vessels, too: the National Maritime Museum, Greenwich, owns a Tomaso de Simone oil painting which depicts the frigate HMS *Liffey* in 1868; a gouache by Antonio de Simone held in the British royal collection portrays several vessels in the Bay of Naples, including the frigate HMS *Doris*.

Previous pages

◆

A Royal Yacht Squadron Schooner off Naples

(Detail)

Tomaso de Simone (active 1850–1900)
(oil on canvas, 44.5 x 66cm, dated 1870)
N R Omell Gallery.

It is believed that Tomaso was the father of Antonio de Simone, who is known for his work in gouache and who signed his pictures simply as 'de Simone'. Tomaso is known for working mostly in oils. This rather static two-dimensional picture lacks the subtlety and atmospheric effects of Antonio de Simone's work. It may be that several hands or studio assistants turned these works out to cater for a rapidly burgeoning market in the second half of the nineteenth century.

On the other side of the world, Anglo-Chinese artists were also painting portraits of visiting yachts (*see page 98*). Like their fellow painters in the Mediterranean, most of these artists remain unknown, although their work regularly appears in sale rooms. Sometimes, Anglo-Chinese portraitists would row out to a yacht with the background harbour and landscape already pre-painted on a canvas. All that was required was to paint in the features of the vessel. Anglo-Chinese yacht portraits often lack the sophistication of western yachting art. The artists generally had little time to produce an accurate description of the vessel, and even less to capture the sea and background detail. Even so, their images are not uninspiring. Many possess subtle lighting effects and have a naive simplicity that gives them great charm.

Most yacht portraitists knew what was expected of them, and they rarely failed to deliver. They normally followed the traditional yacht portrait format, showing the vessel broadside on to display more of its features. Owners liked to think that they were getting value for money and demanded as much nautical detail as possible. For this reason, the yachts are usually portrayed in full sail and on the wave, rather than with sails down, in harbour or dry dock. Figures rarely appear, perhaps because artists considered the inclusion of people as a distraction from the main subject. Many portraitists had reference material to assist them. Some used photographs as *aide-mémoires*, while others studied models of yachts to ensure nautical accuracy. Most portraits were of a small to medium size as they were conceived to hang on bulkheads or in cabins. Larger works were made for yacht clubs or for owners' homes. Occasionally, works were designed for specific spaces, Julius L Stewart's image of the 1866 transatlantic race being an example (*see page 82*).

The ability of artists to create a convincing scene of a particular yacht or yachts racing, with the appropriate rigs, sail arrangements and weather conditions should not be underestimated. What makes the achievements of some of yachting artists even more remarkable is that they were self-taught amateurs. Some were racing captains, master mariners or otherwise professionally associated with the sea. For most amateur artists, a straightforward yacht portrait was testing enough in itself, but some occasionally produced fine examples that rank alongside the best of yachting art.

Thomas Lucop (1834–1906), for instance, was a British master mariner who produced some notable portraits of yachts, including cutter yachts (*see page 95*). Lucop worked as a ship portrait painter and decorator between 1867 and 1906, and he was also a master mariner. Captain J Iddes (active 1850–1890) was a racing captain who lived at Cowes. He painted in oils and watercolour and had first-hand experience of his subjects. He painted the schooner yacht *Livonia* off the Needles. The yacht was built specially for James Ashbury's challenge for the America's Cup in 1871. Unfortunately, she won only one of the five races. Captain Charles Keith Miller (active 1884–1896) also painted competent yachting portraits and races. He was based in Glasgow and exhibited at the Royal Academy of Glasgow in 1888.

Yachting portraitists had to be able to adapt to new emerging markets. Steam yachts were first introduced in the first quarter of the nineteenth century. As well as being popular with ladies, who preferred the more stately progression of steam yachting, steam vessels were better suited for lavish entertaining than sailing yachts. Many were fitted out with extravagant luxury, with large state rooms, elaborate carvings and thick carpets. As an expression of wealth and leisure, the steam yacht appealed greatly to rich owners.

Not everyone approved of the new technology, however. In 1827, the Royal Yacht Squadron at Cowes, for example, passed a resolution barring all steam owners. But by the mid-1840s the club had finally bowed to pressure from the British royal family, whose interest in steam yachts was widely known, and had amended its rule. It did not throw open its doors to all steam yachts, however, but retained certain restrictions: it stated that 'No steamer of less than 100 horse-power shall be qualified for admission into, or entitled to the privileges of, the Squadron.'

The most celebrated steam yachts were often as famous as their owners. The paddle steamer the *North Star*, the first steam yacht to be built in the United States, was owned by 'Commodore' Cornelius Vanderbilt. Launched in 1853 at a cost of $90,000, she had ten luxurious state apartments. In the same year, she set off with Vanderbilt's family on a cruise of the Mediterranean, Scandinavia and the Baltic. The financier John Pierpoint Morgan owned three steam yachts, all called *Corsair*. The first was purchased from a member of the New York Yacht Club in 1882. In 1930, some seventeen years after Morgan's death, the family acquired a fourth yacht of the same name. She survived until the end of the Second World War.

Owners of steam yachts were just as proud of their vessels as owners of sailing yachts, and were equally keen to have their boats painted. In around 1896, one of Morgan's partners, Anthony J Drexel, commissioned the British artist Barlow Brass Moore (active 1863–1900) to paint his steam vessel *Margarita*, the second of three yachts he owned of that name (*see page 99*). The third *Margarita* was considered by one yachting reporter to be 'the finest pleasure craft afloat' when she was launched in 1900. She was sumptuously fitted out and boasted a veritable treasure trove of antiques and paintings. Moore was both a member and the official painter of the Royal Thames Yacht Club. He was also marine painter to two other British royal yacht clubs, the Royal Victoria and the Royal London. The artist was known for his detailed and carefully designed pictures, which he usually executed in watercolour. His depictions of sailing yachts, such as the *Latona*, are equally impressive.

Although interest in yachting was at first slower to grow in the United States than in Britain, by the third quarter of the nineteenth century the sport had expanded rapidly across the country. The Boston Boat Club, established in 1834, is traditionally credited as being the first yacht club in America, but the most famous American yachting society is the New York Yacht Club, founded in 1844 by nine local owners. The growth of the sport was such that between 1857 and 1871 clubs had also been established at Brooklyn, New Orleans, Long Island, Boston and San Francisco.

The American clubs, like their European counterparts, were eager to have their yachts and regattas painted. Many English, German and Danish artists, perhaps disillusioned with life in Europe and looking for new challenges and experiences, emigrated to America and established themselves as marine painters. Chicago, situated at the base of the Great Lakes, is one of many prominent American cities with a thriving interest in yachting. The Chicago Yacht Club was founded in 1875 and today has two club houses and more than 1,750 members. Of the large number of marine painters to be associated with the Great Lakes, William Torgerson (active 1873–1890) stands out as a painter of general shipping and yachting subjects (*see page 98*). The New Brunswick Pier Head artist William Gay Yorke (1817–*c.*1886) is known for his ship portraits and for being the father of William Howard Yorke (1847–1921), who worked in Liverpool where he enjoyed considerable patronage. Both artists painted yachts, and occasionally regattas (*see page 100*). William Gay Yorke lived aboard a small boat, his 'floating studio', which provided him with ready access to his favourite subjects.

Elisha Taylor Baker (1827–1890) ranks as one of America's leading yacht portraitists. He was born in New York City, where his first job was as a fishmonger. Although his business cards describe him as an 'artist' and a 'marine painter', the scarcity of his paintings indicates that he probably took on other work, such as interior decoration. One directory lists him under 'Paper-hangings'. By the end of the Civil War, he had settled in Brooklyn. Baker's paintings are sometimes a little stiff in execution. However, his carefully patterned and sensitively coloured skies and cloud formations are skilfully rendered and recall the work of James Edward Buttersworth. Baker's effulgent lighting effects are also reminiscent of the so-called 'luminist' paintings of Fitz Hugh Lane. In addition to yachts under sail (*see page 101*), Baker also painted sailing ships and vessels powered by steam (*see page 100*), as well as seascapes and harbour scenes, usually showing New York Harbour.

Many American artists were also travelling to Europe to paint, in particular to Britain, where there continued to be a ready market for yacht portraiture, especially in the major ports. Several American artists settled for a time in Liverpool, the main gateway for transatlantic trade. William Jacob Hays (1830–1875), for example, painted a cutter yacht of the Royal Yacht Squadron during a visit to England in around 1860 (*see page 102*). Also born in New York City, Hays studied under John Reubens Smith and became an associate member of the National Academy in New York. His work is represented in the Peabody Museum in Salem, Massachusetts.

The Peabody Museum also owns three oil paintings by Marshall Johnson (1850–1921) (*see page 103*), as well as some of his sketchbooks. The same museum has examples of the work of the relatively obscure German-American artist Conrad Freitag (1845–1894). Freitag is vastly superior to the bulk of yacht portraitists. He had the rare talent of combining careful draughtsmanship with subtle lighting effects. His pictures are fresh and have a spontaneous quality. They may lack the colour of Fitz Hugh Lane's and James Edward Buttersworth's work, but they are certainly not monotonous or dull (*see page 102*). Freitag's style is progressive in that it foreshadows the new realism popularised in the early years of the twentieth century by, among others, the Italian artist Chevalier Eduardo de Martino.

THE CUTTER YACHT
AMPHITRITE

Arthur Wellington Fowles (1815–1883)
(oil on canvas, 51 x 76cm, dated 1879)
Vallejo Maritime Gallery.

The identity of this vessel is not known. However, in 1862, a 52-ton cutter of the name *Amphitrite* was owned by E N Harvey. By 1866, she had been sold to Reverend J N Palmer from Southampton. The yacht in this picture is depicted off the Needles, the famous landmark off the west end of the Isle of Wight.

Fowles also painted naval battles and is known to have produced marine paintings as part of interior decoration schemes for private homes and public houses on the Isle of Wight.

A CUTTER YACHT
CRUISING IN
THE SOLENT

Thomas Lucop (1834–1906)
(oil on canvas, 39.5 x 59.5cm, dated 1885)
N R Omell Gallery.

As a master mariner, Lucop had first-hand experience of the sea. He also worked as a ship portrait painter and decorator in Hull. Examples of his work can be found at the Ferens Art Gallery in Hull. He occasionally signed his work 'Lucup'. The style of this portrait of an unidentified yacht is reminiscent of the work of the American artists William Gay Yorke and Antonio Jacobsen. Ship portraits and yachting scenes by the little-known master mariner Captain J W Anderson (exhibited 1857–1865) often appear at auctions.

ROYAL ALBERT YACHT CLUB 20-TON MATCH, 1882
(Detail)

John Horner (active 1870–1890)
(watercolour, 23.5 x 37cm, circa 1882)
N R Omell Gallery.

In 1882, the Royal Albert Yacht Club, established in 1865 and based in Southsea, was host to a 20-ton match between the yachts *Buttercup*, owned by Robert Hewitt, *Katie*, owned by W W Pilkington, *Freja*, owned by Herbert A Salwey, and *Amethea*, owned by W W MacLellan.

Signed either 'FH' or 'JH', this is probably the work of John Horner of London, who exhibited several works at the Suffolk Street Gallery between 1881 and 1886. He produced figure portraits, architectural scenes, landscapes and marine paintings. In this work, Horner has focused on the sail arrangements of the racing yachts to create a visually striking composition.

John Horner is traditionally believed to have painted works for Queen Victoria. P J Ouless (1817–1885), Reverend H J Vernon (active 1850s), W E Atkins (c. 1842–1910) and W F Mitchell (1845–1914) are among the many other marine artists who painted for the queen.

A ROYAL YACHT SQUADRON STEAM YACHT IN HONG KONG HARBOUR

Nineteenth-Century Anglo-Chinese School
(oil on canvas, 39.5 x 52cm, circa 1865)
N R Omell Gallery.

This is an unidentified yacht of the Royal Yacht Squadron painted by an unknown Anglo-Chinese artist. Although Hong Kong was a favourite stopover for yachts, it was not until 1889 that the Royal Hong Kong Yacht Club was founded.

Many Anglo-Chinese portraits have a somewhat two-dimensional appearance, and are uninspiring in terms of design. The sea, for instance, is often crudely denoted by a succession of fluid brush strokes. However, some examples of a more sophisticated appearance have survived and these are full of local colour and detail. This work is unusual in that it does not portray the vessel in full sail.

YACHTS RACING ON THE GREAT LAKES

William Torgerson (active 1873–1890)
(oil on canvas laid down on board,
56 x 91.5cm, circa 1880)
Vallejo Maritime Gallery.

In this richly coloured, unusual head-on view, a sloop and two schooners, wearing the burgee of the Oconomowoc Yacht Club of Wisconsin, are portrayed contesting an unrecorded race. Spectators are following the race in one of the Great Lakes excursion steamers.

Little is known about this artist, who was almost certainly of Scandinavian origin but based in the United States. He is known to have provided designs for the Cunard Steamship Company, which were produced into lithographic prints. Torgerson's work rarely comes onto the market. There are examples in the Chicago Historical Society and the Boston Museum of Fine Arts.

THE *MARGARITA II* OFF GIBRALTAR, 1896

Barlow Brass Moore (active 1863–1900)
(oil on canvas, 61 x 101.5cm, dated 1896)
Vallejo Maritime Gallery.

In this highly colourful work, Barlow Brass Moore has portrayed the celebrated American steam yacht *Margarita II* surrounded by a number of local craft. The American banker Anthony J Drexel owned three yachts named *Margarita*. The first was designed by A H Brown and built by Ramage & Ferguson in 1889. G L Watson, famous for his design of the British royal racing yacht *Britannia*, designed the second *Margarita*. The 1,332-ton yacht was built at Lord Ailsa's Ailsa Shipbuilding Company at Troon and launched in 1896. *Margarita III* was also designed by G L Watson and built by Scott & Company at Greenock. She was launched in 1900 at a cost of £100,000. In 1911, she was sold to the Marquis of Anglesey, who renamed her *Semiramis*. She was commissioned into service during the First World War, when her name was changed to *Alacrity*. The yacht also saw active duty in the Second World War.

Moore exhibited at the three principal London art venues: the Royal Academy, the British Institution in Pall Mall, established in 1806 as a rival to the Royal Academy, and the Society of British Artists in Suffolk Street, founded by a group of rebel artists in 1824. Although he painted a number of steam yachts, he was equally adept at portraits of yachts under sail. Today Moore's work can be seen in the Royal Thames Yacht Club.

RACE DAY

William Gay Yorke (1817–c.1886)
(oil on canvas, 56 x 76cm,
circa 1870)
The Kelton Foundation Collection.

William Gay Yorke's painting shows an unrecorded race of the 1870s. Such events created tremendous excitement and it was common for spectators to view them from steamboats and small boats.

Yorke's colourful palette, vigorous and fresh technique, and his eye for nautical detail, made him popular with seafarers, most of whom were undeterred by the absence of artistic refinement. Yorke and his fellow Pier Head artists were painting for captains and masters, ship and yacht owners, not for art galleries or special exhibitions.

A TENDER OF THE SEAWANHAKA CORINTHIAN YACHT CLUB

Elisha Taylor Baker (1827–1890)
(oil on canvas, 30.5 x 56cm, circa 1880)
Hyland Granby Antiques.

The burgee of the second yacht club to be founded in New York, the Seawanhaka Corinthian Yacht Club, flies from the top of the mainmast of this steamboat. It is likely that the vessel was the official club race committee boat. Baker was predominantly interested in working vessels throughout his career. In the background, to the left, are a number of sailing yachts, probably waiting for the race to begin.

A Cutter off a Lighthouse

Elisha Taylor Baker
(oil on canvas, 63.5 x 76cm, circa 1885)
Private Collection.

Even though the flag flying off the leech of this cutter's sail is distinctive, it has not yet been possible to identify the yacht. Baker's surviving paintings reveal that he was a highly gifted yachting artist, but his works are lamentably few in number. This has led Anthony J Peluso Jr, the leading authority on the artist, to point out: 'There is no doubt that he was a fine marine artist, but there is so little over which we can celebrate.'

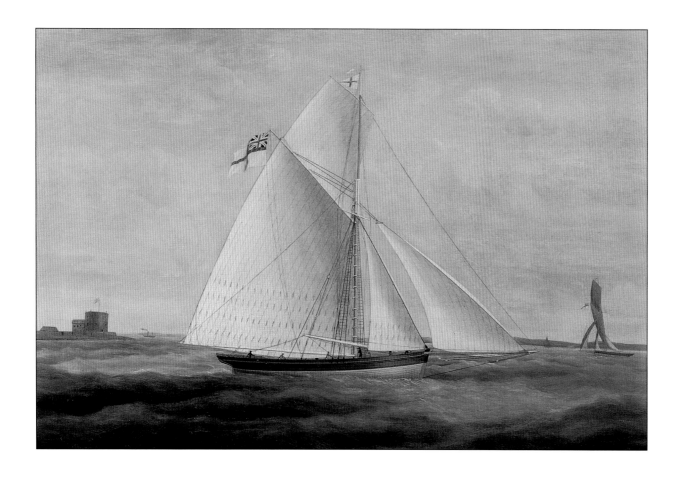

A Cutter Yacht of the Royal Yacht Squadron cruising off Hurst Castle in the Solent

William Jacob Hays (1830-1875)
(oil on canvas, 71 x 101.5cm, circa 1860)
N R Omell Gallery.

This is a classic yacht portrait of the traditional form. Attention has been paid to the yacht's appearance, rigging and sails. In comparison, the sea and topographical details are crudely handled.

William Jacob Hays travelled extensively and undertook a painting trip along the upper Mississippi River in 1860. An example of his work is in the Peabody Museum, Salem, Massachusetts.

The Schooner Yacht *Siren*, 1882

Conrad Freitag (1845-1894)
(oil on canvas, 71 x 106.5cm, circa 1882)
Hyland Granby Antiques.

The yacht *Siren* was 82.6ft in length, 19.1ft in breadth and had a draft of 6.1ft. She was built in New Brunswick in 1874 by Lewis Hoagland for her owner E R Washburn. She was registered to the port of New York and flew the burgee of the New York Yacht Club.

Next to nothing is known about Freitag. Born in Denmark, he arrived in New York City in 1860 and settled in Brooklyn the following year. He exhibited at the National Academy in New York, and at the Brooklyn Art Association between 1874 and 1883.

A CATBOAT UNDER SAIL

Marshall Johnson (1850–1921)
(oil on canvas, 63.5 x 77cm, circa 1890)
Hyland Granby Antiques.

This work by a Boston-born artist is a charming portrait of small sailing boat used for fishing and recreation. The boat appears to be rounding a channel marker.

Marshall Johnson studied at the Lowell Institute in Massachusetts. As a youth, he set off on a sea voyage aboard the ship *Sunbeam* but was shipwrecked.

Fortunately, he was rescued. He went on to become a marine painter, and later studied under William Edward Norton (1843–1916). After his artistic studies, he travelled in Europe and on his return to America, set up his own painting studio in India Wharf, Boston.

CHAPTER VII

The Art of Yachting Illustration

IN THE SECOND HALF OF THE NINETEENTH CENTURY, THERE WAS A GROWING NUMBER OF YACHTING ARTISTS WHO WANTED NOT ONLY TO REPRODUCE ACCURATE NAUTICAL DETAIL BUT ALSO TO ACHIEVE REALISTIC EFFECTS IN THEIR WORK. AT THE SAME TIME, AS YACHTING BECAME INCREASINGLY POPULAR, ARTISTS AND ILLUSTRATORS PRODUCED PAINT- INGS, DRAWINGS AND PRINTS TO HELP EXPLAIN AND DEMONSTRATE THE RULES AND EQUIPMENT OF THE SPORT TO THE GENERAL PUBLIC.

On the whole, yachting artists paint- ed on commission for yacht owners and not for sale in art galleries. This was partly because owners and art connoisseurs tend- ed to have opposing tastes, with yacht por- traitists being generally less highly regarded as mere 'documentary recorders' in comparison with their peers whose work was deemed 'art'. However, as real- ism became more common in art in gener- al during the second half of the nineteenth century, those yachting artists who could combine nautical accuracy with a convinc- ing portrayal of the vessel moving through the water, and who could paint authentic seas and skies, as well as conveying other naturalistic effects, were in greater demand. These artists were able to sell their work in galleries because their pictures were seen as a combination of record and art.

The artist who did the most to bring a new realism to yachting art was Eduardo Federico de Martino (1838–1912). Although relatively unknown today, he deserves to be acknowledged as one of the leading painters of the genre. His paintings have a boldness, freshness and verve that have rarely been surpassed. De Martino was born in 1838 in Meta, then part of the Kingdom of Naples. His family were seafarers. Destined to follow in the footsteps of his

Previous pages

◆

YACHTS OF THE BIG CLASS RACING
(Detail)

Charles Dixon (1872-1934)
(watercolour heightened with white, 54.5 x 76cm, dated 1934)
Collection of HRH the Duke of Edinburgh.

In this stunning and dramatic close-up action picture, the black hull of the royal racing yacht *Britannia* can be seen almost in the centre of the picture as she takes part in this J-class race in the early 1930s. Dixon expertly conveys the sensation of speed. The vessel to the left is almost certainly T O M Sopwith's *Endeavour*, designed and built by Charles Nicholson in 1934.

Born in Goring-on-Thames, Oxfordshire, England, Charles Dixon was the son of the genre and history painter Alfred Dixon. He painted yachting scenes and naval subjects. He also produced cover illustrations for yachting magazines. Dixon often produced large-format paintings, but he worked quickly, completing each picture in a very short time. He first exhibited at the Royal Academy in 1889, and had works shown there most years. Dixon's favourite medium was watercolour and he was a member of the New Watercolour Society. He also worked in oils, however. One of his best-known oil paintings is *Queen Victoria Diamond Jubilee Review at Spithead, 26 July 1897*, which is now in the National Maritime Museum, Greenwich.

father, who had been a chief pilot in the British Royal Navy, Eduardo studied at the Naval Academy in Naples. At the same time, he also attended classes at the city's Institute of Fine Arts. His naval career proved to be short-lived, however, and he soon turned his full attention towards marine painting, first at Montevideo in Uruguay, then at Porto Alego in Brazil. Having cultivated his excellent naval contacts, the artist was introduced to the Brazilian emperor Pedro II who, in recognition of his ser- vices, made him a Cavaliere of the Order of the Rose. He thus became commonly known as the Chevalier de Martino.

During the 1870s, de Martino mar- ried and moved to St John's Wood in London, which at the time was a fashion- able artists' colony. His love of yachting and high social standing soon brought him to the attention of the Prince of Wales – the future Edward VII – with whom he formed a close friendship. De Martino was acclaimed for his ability to make quick sketches. While on board the British royal yacht *Osborne* in September 1898, he made a sketch of the yacht on the back of a menu card and inscribed the words: 'To the Captain of the best Royal Yacht in the World.' This sketch and similar works by de Martino are held in the National Maritime Museum, Greenwich. One of the artist's finest yachting pictures, which shows *Columbia* and *Shamrock* off Sandy Hook, October, 1899 (*see page 110*), now hangs over the bar of the New York Yacht Club. In addition to yachts, he also painted many naval scenes, reviews and state occasions.

According to Roberto Romano, a specialist on the artist, de Martino was an exceptionally proud man. But he also apparently lacked confidence in his own abilities. He never submitted a painting to the Royal Academy of Arts in London for fear of rejection. Despite his self-doubt, de Martino achieved widespread acclaim during his career. He succeeded Sir Oswald Walter Brierly as the honorary marine painter to the Royal Yacht Squadron from 1895 until 1912, and through his contact with the British royal family, he received commissions and decorations from several heads of state and European royalty.

De Martino had a novel way of coping with the large amount of commissions that he received from yacht designers, owners, yachtsmen and clubs. He employed John Fraser (1858–1927) (*see page 110*) to paint the actual pictures on his behalf, which he then signed and passed off as his own. Occasionally, de Martino might paint a finishing touch, such as a flag or another minor detail, but otherwise the work was entirely Fraser's. In de Martino's defence, he had the excuse of ill health. He had suffered a stroke in 1879 which had weakened his right side, making the painting process slow and painful.

A startling contrast to de Martino's grand composition of the America's Cup race of 1899 is the remarkable collage of the same subject by Thomas Willis (1850–1912) (*see page 111*). Willis was of Danish-Irish extraction; his name was originally spelt 'Willes'. He emigrated to the United States in 1870, and settled in Brooklyn, where he was employed in the manufacture and sale of silk thread. He set up his own business in 1880 and developed a wide clientele of yacht owners and clubs, among whom his unique works of art were in plentiful demand. He produced several colourful relief collages of yacht portraits and races, sometimes using a variety of different materials, such as silk, velvet, embroidery and oil paints, on the same picture. Willis's works are now highly sought after by maritime collectors.

Willis was just one of many European marine artists who settled in America during the latter part of the nineteenth century. These included Charles Sidney Raleigh (1830–1925), who painted various portraits of the America's Cup yachts (*see page 112*). Brewington's *Dictionary of Marine Artists* is the major source on this gifted artist. Raleigh was born in Gloucester, southwest England. It is traditionally believed that he ran away from home, and arrived in America on board a British naval ship.

For a time, he was a merchant seaman before working as a decorator and house painter in New Bedford, Massachusetts. Raleigh's paintings possess an appealing crispness, achieved through his design and use of a light palette. Examples of Raleigh's pictures can now be found in the Kendall Whaling Museum, the Mariners' Museum, Newport News, and at Mystic Seaport.

Although the Danish-American painter Antonio Jacobsen (1850–1921) lacked the royal support, aristocratic connections and artistic versatility of Eduardo Federico de Martino, he nonetheless enjoyed a much greater popular following in his day than the Neapolitan artist. Originally from Copenhagen, Jacobsen was born into a talented musical family. In 1873, he arrived in New York, where he briefly played in an orchestra. He was then employed by the Marvin Safe Company to decorate safes with flowers. He was drawn into maritime painting when a ship broker requested that he paint a maritime scene on his safe rather than a floral design. A wealthy patron noticed his work and gave him his first major ship portrait commission.

Jacobsen quickly established himself as one of the leading ship portraitists in America, recording the period of transition from sail to steam. By the late 1880s, the artist and his family were living in West Hoboken, New Jersey, where they socialised with fellow artists such as the ship portraitist James Bard (1815–1897), James Edward Buttersworth and the celebrated maritime illustrator Frederick Schiller Cozzens (1856–1928). Jacobsen turned out numerous pot-boilers, and to date more than six thousand examples of his work have been recorded. Although his portraits of steamships crossing the Atlantic, painted in gouache and oils, are of an uneven quality, his yachting subjects, mostly early works painted in the 1870s and 1880s, are highly valued today. His finest work combines an accurate knowledge of shipping and attention to realistic atmospheric conditions, but it is his bold compositions and vigorous seas for which he is most admired (*see pages 112 and 114–5*).

Charles Gulager (1826–1899) was another gifted marine artist of Danish descent. Although next to nothing is known about his life, he is well represented in American museums. Gulager's studio was located in Philadelphia, where he exhibited several pictures at the Pennsylvania

Academy of Art. Most of his recorded yachting works were exhibited in the 1860s. His compositions lack the forceful nature of Antonio Jacobsen, but they are nonetheless characterised by the graceful subtlety of his atmospheric effects (*see page 113*).

Originally from Bolton in Lancashire, Edward Moran (1829–1901) also travelled to America to paint yachting pictures. He was taught by the Philadelphia-based marine artist James Hamilton. He also studied in Europe, first at the Royal Academy in London and later in Paris, before returning to New York in 1871. Moran shared his master's passion for the paintings of J M W Turner. Like Turner's work, Moran's style is noteworthy for its spectacular lighting and atmospheric effects and its bold strokes of colour (*see page 116*).

Frederick Schiller Cozzens is perhaps best known for his detailed watercolours and lithographs of the America's Cup races, executed at the end of the nineteenth century and the beginning of the twentieth. As one would expect from an illustrator, his depiction of the first America's Cup race is a more literal representation than that of Moran. Cozzens displays a masterly command of draughtsmanship and nautical detail, and an intuitive grasp of how to arrange his subjects in the clear and legible manner required for illustrations.

Cozzens was born in Livingston on Staten Island, New York, where his father worked as a wine merchant and writer. After graduating from Rensselaer Polytechnic in 1867, he became a professional artist. He soon won the admiration of both yachtsmen and yacht designers. He was often commissioned directly by the owners of vessels, and it is known that the Rhode Island designer Nathaniel Herreshoff was also an admirer of his work. By 1883, Cozzens was well established as a leading maritime artist. He then embarked on a series of yachting prints that would ensure him a steady income. His first set of prints, *American Yachts: Their Clubs and Races*, was a series of twenty-seven full-colour designs that was published by Charles Scribner & Sons in New York in 1884. The preparatory watercolours for the series are now collectors' items. They are widely acknowledged by both the yachting and artistic fraternities as being among the finest examples of yachting art ever produced (*see page 113*). Because Cozzens worked quickly and used thin

washes of watercolour sometimes heightened with white, his range of colour was muted, which has led some critics to believe that his work has faded due to prolonged light exposure.

In addition to yachting subjects, Cozzens also depicted ship portraits and naval scenes. *Harper's Bazaar*, *The Daily Graphic*, *Yachts and Yachting* and *Our Navy* were among the many newspapers and magazines to publish his illustrations. He also wrote and illustrated several books, including *American Yachts and Yachting*, published by Cassell & Compass in 1888. In this classic work, Cozzens created deceptively simple line drawings, mostly prepared in 1886, that are remarkable for their economy of description. Cozzens knew how to strip his subject down to the bare essentials. His draughtsmanship is uncluttered and never overworked. He exhibits a lighter side of his nature in his vignettes illustrating life at sea during a yacht race. One line drawing, entitled *I don't care a — who wins*, for instance, shows a young, unfortunate sailor suffering from a bad case of seasickness.

The Scottish maritime artist and illustrator Henry Shields (active 1870–1904) also benefited from the burgeoning market for yachting art and illustration. Although he showed less talent than Cozzens, he prepared many designs for yachting subjects that were made into chromolithographic prints. Some of his original watercolours, for instance, were published as chromolithographs in *Famous Clyde Yachts 1880–87*. The work contained descriptive notices by James Meikle, author of *Yachting Yarns and Clydeside Sketches*, and was published by Oatts & Runciman in Glasgow and London in 1888. Shields exhibited his oil paintings in Glasgow.

In the late 1800s and early 1900s, several maritime artists were employed as roving 'visual journalists' by the illustrated weekly newspapers, notably the *Illustrated London News*. This publication, which was established in 1842, supplied its readers with a mix of illustrated reports, stories and articles on a wide range of subjects, such as politics, wars and insurrections and high-society functions. As yachting grew in popularity, the public was keen to follow the progress of the high-profile races, especially the America's Cup challenges. Recognising the widespread interest in yachting features, the *Illustrated London News* reported all the major events, its artists providing visual accounts of the proceedings (*see page 119*). It also printed explanatory illustrations and diagrams which were designed to educate the general reader in the rules and equipment of the sport. The newspaper was very successful – it is still published today – and many similar publications soon followed its lead, including *The Graphic* and *The Sphere*. At first, illustrations for the weekly newspapers were produced by general wood engravers, who were expected to turn their hand to any subject. Later, however, as readers demanded more accurate and realistic representations, specialist professional illustrators were employed instead.

As a result, some of the best-known yachting artists worked for the illustrated weekly newspapers. Edward John Gregory (1850–1909) and William Lionel Wyllie (1851–1931), for example, both worked for *The Graphic*. Wyllie drew and painted every conceivable type of maritime subject, and from the 1870s he provided illustrations of yachting and naval scenes. *The Sphere* employed both the Australian artist Arthur James Weatherall Burgess (1879–1957), who by 1901 had settled in London, and Montague Dawson (1895–1973), arguably the most popular maritime painter of the twentieth century. For a time, the *Illustrated London News* employed Charles John de Lacy (*c.*1860–1936), whose contacts with the army and navy were another useful source of commissions for the artist. In 1910, Charles Murray Padday (*c.*1870–1954) provided a unique series of illustrations explaining yacht-racing rules for the publication; some of the preparatory designs in monochrome have survived to this day (*see page 118*). Padday also painted and drew rare close-up deck scenes that expressed the carefree fun and excitement of small-boat yachting in Edwardian Britain before the outbreak of the First World War in 1914 brought the sport in the country to a complete standstill (*see page 117*).

Charles Dixon (1872–1934), Cecil King (1881–1942), Frank Henry Mason (1876–1965) and Norman Wilkinson (1878–1971) all worked as illustrators for the *Illustrated London News* at some point in their careers. Charles Dixon was born into an artistic family. He was probably taught by his father, who was a traditional historical painter. As well as working for the *Illustrated London News*, Dixon was also employed by *The Sphere* and *The Graphic*. He painted naval actions and reviews but is best known today for his watercolours of working boats and sailing ships on the River Thames. He also had a lifelong passion for yachts, however. In particular, he recorded his friend Sir Thomas Lipton's attempts with his various *Shamrock* yachts to regain the America's Cup. He also painted some of the first portraits of the early J-class yachts of the 1930s (*see page 104–5*). He exhibited at the New Watercolour Society and the Royal Academy in London.

Cecil King was the *Illustrated London News*'s official naval artist in the Baltic Sea during the 1914–18 war. King studied at Goldsmiths' College and Westminster Art School in London, and also in Paris. He was a founder member of the Society of Marine Artists. He exhibited at the Royal Academy and was appointed honorary marine painter to the Royal Thames Yacht Club in 1932.

Norman Wilkinson was sent to New York by the *Illustrated London News* to cover Sir Thomas Lipton's second attempt to win the America's Cup. His sketches were sent back to London and worked up by A C Seppings Wright, one of the stable of in-house designers employed by the *Illustrated London News*. Wilkinson continued to work for the paper until 1915. He was an enthusiastic yachtsman and was made honorary marine painter to the Royal Yacht Squadron in 1919.

By the 1930s, the market for yachting illustrations for illustrated periodicals had virtually disappeared. With the widespread use of commercial photography, the illustrated newspapers were now largely dependent on photographs to portray yachts in action. Some of the finest yachting illustrators remained popular, however. The English artists George Horace Davis (1881–1963) and Charles E Turner (1883–1965), for instance, made their reputations with carefully crafted technical designs and detailed cut-through drawings, which made potentially complicated subjects, such as the sail arrangement and rig of a yacht, considerably easier to comprehend for the uninformed layman. Davis's 'visual explanation' of *Endeavour I*'s sail plan and rigging (*see page 119*) is a masterly piece of yachting design. The illustration appeared in the *Illustrated London News* in 1934, just as yachting was reaching its golden age.

THE OLD TRAIL

John Fraser (1858–1927)
(oil on canvas, 96.5 x 170cm, dated 1913)
N R Omell Gallery.

The schooner yacht *America* is seen here off the Lizard. The yacht survived until 1945, when she was destroyed after the shed temporarily housing her in Annapolis, Maryland collapsed during a snowstorm. Even so, she remains one of the most popular subjects for marine painters to this day.

John Fraser came from a London nautical family. In 1885, he sailed to North America, and for the next twenty years he travelled the world. His realistic style is indebted to Thomas Somerscales who may have been his master, and also to some extent to Eduardo de Martino. Fraser exhibited at the Royal Academy between 1885 and 1919.

COLUMBIA AND *SHAMROCK I* OFF SANDY HOOK, OCTOBER 1899

Chevalier Eduardo de Martino (1838–1912)
(oil on canvas, 75 x 166cm, dated 1906)
New York Yacht Club.

This painting depicts the tenth series for the America's Cup, in which the New York Yacht Club's defender, *Columbia*, defeated the Royal Ulster Yacht Club's challenger, *Shamrock I*, the first of five yachts of that name owned by Sir Thomas Lipton.

The artist de Martino witnessed and recorded the race. To the right of centre of his painting is the black-hulled steam yacht *Corsair III*. In 1899, John Pierpoint Morgan became Commodore of the New York Yacht Club and appointed *Corsair III* as the club's flagship. In fact, it may have been J P Morgan who commissioned this picture, which now hangs over the bar of the New York Yacht Club.

Astern of the *Corsair* is the yellow funnel and white hull of Sir Thomas Lipton's steam yacht *Erin*. She was built in 1896 as the *Aegusa* and was used as an escort for Lipton's racing yachts. De Martino was familiar with this luxurious yacht and his watercolours adorned its bulkheads.

COLUMBIA AND *SHAMROCK I*, AMERICA'S CUP, OCTOBER 1899

Thomas Willis (1850–1912)
(oil on canvas, silk, velvet and embroidery, 46 x 81cm, circa 1899)
Vallejo Maritime Gallery.

Shamrock I is seen here trailing behind the Nathaniel Herreshoff-designed *Columbia*. The American yacht was owned by a syndicate led by the Morgan family and skippered by Charlie Barr. Lipton did not give up easily and he made four consecutive attempts to win the America's Cup, all of which failed. George Watson replaced William Fife as the designer of *Shamrock II* for the 1901 series. Two years later, William Fife was given another chance. For the attempts in 1920 and 1930, Charles Nicholson was the chosen designer.

In Thomas Willis's collage, the hulls of the yachts are made of velvet with embroidered decks, spars and rigging. The sails are made of silk. Featured on each vessel are embroidered figures.

PORTRAIT OF THE YACHT *COLUMBIA* UNDER SAIL

Charles Sidney Raleigh (1830–1925)
(oil on canvas, 76 x 107cm, dated 1908)
Hyland Granby Antiques.

Columbia was again selected as the defender of the America's Cup in 1901. She was skippered once more by Charlie Barr. Lipton's challenger was *Shamrock II*. She was beaten in all three races.

Raleigh has taken great pains to paint the yacht's crew. The dramatic sky and handling of the clouds are reminiscent of James Edward Buttersworth, with whose work Raleigh would have been familiar.

THE YACHT *PURITAN*

Antonio Jacobsen (1850–1921)
(oil on canvas, 56 x 91.5cm, dated 1885)
Hyland Granby Antiques.

This work is one of a rare pair of portraits showing the America's Cup yachts, the only recorded pair of yachting portraits painted by Jacobsen. The companion portrait depicts Sir Richard Sutton's *Genesta*. The *Puritan* was 94ft in length, 22ft 7in in beam and had a draft of 8ft 8in. She raced against the *Priscilla*, *Bedouin* and *Gracie* for the right to defend the America's Cup in 1885. *Puritan* was selected after these trials, and ultimately went on to win the cup itself.

THE SCHOONER *MAGIC*

Charles Gulager (1826–1899)
(oil on canvas, 91.5 x 137cm, dated 1860)
Vallejo Maritime Gallery.

Magic is seen here racing against the sloop *Maria*, shown astern with other yachts. The painting was commissioned by her owner R F Loper of Philadelphia. Originally designed by Loper as a sloop and called *Madgie*, she was built by Byerly & Son in 1857. She was converted to a schooner and renamed in 1859. *Magic* was one of the most acclaimed yachts of the nineteenth century, and is best remembered as the winner of the first defence of the America's Cup in 1870.

This large-scale painting is skilfully crafted. Gulager's draughtsmanship is accomplished and he clearly had a detailed knowledge of his subject.

A BREEZY DAY OUTSIDE

Frederick Schiller Cozzens (1846–1928)
(watercolour on paper, 35.5 x 51cm, circa 1884)
Private Collection.

BY SOU'WEST SPIT

Frederick Schiller Cozzens
(watercolour on paper, 35.5 x 51cm, dated 1883)
Private Collection.

The yachts featured in this carefully drawn design are, from left to right, *Columbia*, *Sappho* and *Palmer*. This design featured as Plate XVII of Cozzen's celebrated chromolithographic series, 'American Yachts', published in 1884.

The New York Yacht Club selected four yachts to defend the America's Cup in 1871. Of the four, *Columbia* and *Sappho* were raced. Franklin Osgood's *Columbia* was skippered by J B van Deusen. In the third race, she was partly disabled in heavy weather and was beaten by *Livonia*, of the Royal Harwich Yacht Club.

This design was translated into Plate XIII of 'American Yachts'. The yachts shown are *Roamar*, *Clytie*, *Grayling*, *Fanita* and *Crocodile*. *Clytie* represented both the Seawanhaka and the Atlantic Yacht Clubs, and while the New York Yacht Club was the leading representative of American yachting, the two junior organisations also had yachts worthy of entering any contest.

The preferred course on Lower New York Bay left Buoy 10 on Sou'West Spit to port Buoy 8½ off Sandy Hook also to port, around Sandy Hook lightship and then back to finish the course off Fort Wandsworth where the Narrows of New York Harbour commence.

GRAYLING LEADS AT THE MARK
(Detail)

Antonio Jacobsen
(oil on canvas, 61 x 107cm, dated 1888)
Vallejo Maritime Gallery.

This painting, widely regarded as one of the Danish-born American artist's masterpieces, portrays four of the early America's Cup contenders, *Grayling, Magic, Dauntless* and *Alarm*, during the New York Yacht Club's regatta in the autumn of 1888. The yachts wear the burgee of the club and are shown approaching the buoy that marked one leg of the 30-mile course. Luffing her giant Queen-Fisherman staysail, *Grayling* has already taken the lead by the time the yachts reach this mark. She eventually triumphed.

THE AMERICA'S CUP RACE OF 1871

Edward Moran (1829–1901)
(oil on canvas, 56 x 94cm, circa 1882)
Vallejo Maritime Gallery.

Having failed with *Cambria* to win the first challenge for the America's Cup, James Ashbury tried again in 1871, this time with the schooner yacht *Livonia*, designed by Michael Ratsey. Moran's powerful composition captures the drama and excitement of the occasion. *Livonia* is trying to overtake the 134ft New York Yacht Club defender *Sappho*, designed by C & R Poillon, and skippered by Sam Greenwood. The second America's Cup again ultimately ended in disappointment for Britain.

SAILING IN

Frank Henry Mason (1876–1965)
(oil on canvas,
51 x 61cm, circa 1950)
Vallejo Maritime Gallery.

The crew of the yacht in the foreground watch the arrival of the Australian ketch with keen interest.

Mason was a painter, illustrator and poster designer. He was educated on the training ship HMS *Conway* and served in the Royal Naval Volunteer Reserve as a commissioned artist during the First World War. He exhibited at the Royal Academy.

Mason's style, along with that of his contemporary Charles Robert Paterson (1878–1958), has influenced the work of the popular American marine artist David Bareford (b. 1947), who paints the America's Cup yachts and yachting scenes at Martha's Vineyard.

EDWARDIAN YACHTS RACING

Charles Murray Padday (c.1870–1954)
(oil on canvas, 46 x 66cm, circa *1910)*
Royal Exchange Art Gallery.

The woman shown at the helm in this Edwardian yachting scene is believed to be
Sheila, Duchess of Westminster, who won an Olympic bronze medal in 1908.
The navigator, Major Sir Philip Hunloke, became King George V's sailing master
and was Commodore of the Royal Yacht Squadron from 1943 to 1947.

Padday's carefully described tonal composition sums up yachting in the
Edwardian era. Notice the worn varnish on the deck in the foreground. The artist
has also omitted to paint the feet of the helmsman.

A YACHT ASHORE

Charles Murray Padday
(monochrome on canvas board, 30.5 x 40.5cm, circa 1910)
National Maritime Museum, Greenwich.

An inscription below this picture indicates that Padday has illustrated one of the yacht racing rules as they were in around 1910. The inscription reads: 'Rule 36 – Running ashore – A yacht grounding may use her own anchors and spars – any gear must be restored before she continues the race.' Today the organisation, conduct and judging of the sport are governed by the International Yacht Racing Rules, established by the International Yacht Racing Union and updated every four years.

Padday lived most of his life in the south of England, first on Hayling Island in Hampshire, and later at Cuckfield in Sussex. He tended to paint coastal scenes, historical subjects and landscapes. Padday was the *Illustrated London News'* leading maritime illustrator from 1896 to 1916. He excelled at yachting subjects and was an unofficial painter to several yacht clubs. He exhibited fifteen works at the Royal Academy between 1890 and 1904. When he died, he left effects valued at £2,843. 7s. Although this was not a fortune, it reflected a relatively successful career.

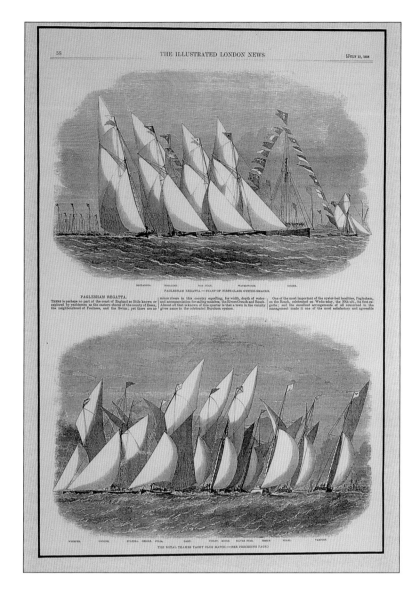

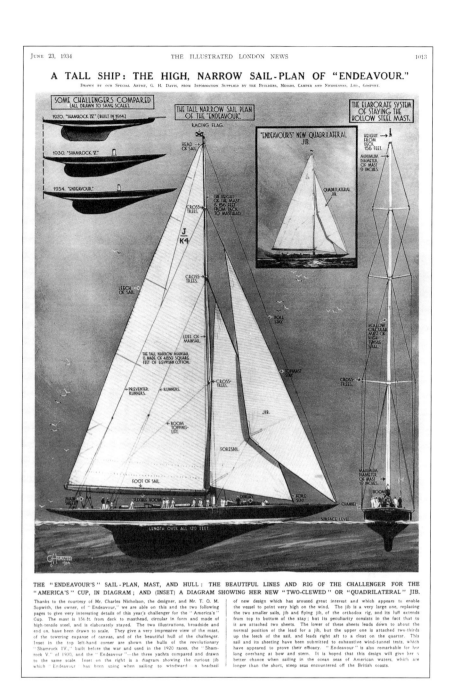

THE PAGLESHAM REGATTA: THE START OF THE FIRST-CLASS OYSTER RACE (*TOP*), AND THE ROYAL THAMES YACHT CLUB MATCH (*BELOW*)

Joseph Robert Wells (active 1850s–1893)
(wood engravings, 38 x 25.5cm, published 17 July 1858)
Illustrated London News.

These illustrations are typical examples of the wood engravings used by the illustrated weekly newspapers until photography became popular in the late 1890s. Sometimes the engraver also prepared the original design, but usually he worked from sketches provided by artists who had actually witnessed the yacht races or events. Around the year 1900, photographs were beginning to replace drawings as the principal form of illustration. In fact, the first popular daily picture-paper, the *Daily Graphic*, was started in 1890.

Joseph Robert Wells was the principal artist of the the *Illustrated London News* from 1873 to 1883, specialising in maritime subjects, especially ship portraits.

A TALL SHIP: THE HIGH, NARROW SAIL-PLAN OF *ENDEAVOUR*

George Horace Davis (1881–1963)
(monochrome illustration, 42 x 29.5cm, published 23 June 1934)
Illustrated London News.

Charles Nicholson designed *Endeavour I* for T O M Sopwith's challenge for the America's Cup in 1934. Unfortunately, she lost 4-2 to *Rainbow*, skippered by Harold Vanderbilt. *Endeavour* is drawn here by one of the *Illustrated London News'* illustrators, George Horace Davis. He worked from information supplied by the builders, Camper & Nicholson. Note how, although the illustration appeared in a magazine aimed at a general reader, it shows the yacht in great technical detail. This provides some indication of the widespread interest in yachting during the 1930s.

CHAPTER VIII

The Golden Age of Yachting

Around the turn of the century, designers in both Britain and the United States were building larger and faster yachts than ever before. These big-class racing vessels attracted huge public attention, and the sport grew amazingly in popularity in the years leading up to the First World War.

Although the outbreak of fighting in 1914 brought all yachting in the belligerent countries to a standstill, immediately after the war there was an attempt to restart big-class racing. In 1920, the America's Cup race between *Shamrock IV* and *Resolute*, which had been cancelled in 1914, was finally contested; in 1923, the Bermuda races from New York to the island of Bermuda were resumed; and in 1925 the first Fastnet race from Cowes round the Fastnet rock off south-west Ireland to Plymouth, took place. The race led to the formation of the Ocean Racing Club, which became the Royal Ocean Racing Club six years later and the governing authority of offshore racing in Britain.

In 1925, an international conference was held, at which a new measurement rule was agreed that gave designers a certain degree of freedom in relation to the size and form of the yachts. It was under this rule that the big J-class racing yachts were built. These were perhaps the greatest of all yacht designs, but they lasted less than twenty years. By 1937, the rising costs of building, maintaining and racing the vessels made them too expensive except for the very wealthy.

With their graceful lines and vast areas of sail, the J-class yachts attracted the attention of many yachting artists. William Lionel Wyllie had a passionate interest in the sea and all its activities, and he often painted the big-class vessels. He would paint and sketch from his yacht *Ladybird*, built specially for him in Boulogne. For a time, he and his wife Marion lived on board, in the yacht's remarkably cramped conditions. *Ladybird* was used extensively for cruising on the continent, especially to France and Holland, and was of great use in bringing Wyllie into contact with new maritime sub-

Previous pages

◆

'Britannia's Glory'
The Royal Yacht *Victoria*
and *Albert III* off Cowes
(*Detail*)

Arthur James Weatherall Burgess (1879-1957)
(oil on panel, 45 x 55cm, dated 1905)
Tryon & Swann Gallery. Reproduced by permission
of Stephen Bartley.

Cowes, on the Isle of Wight, is the headquarters of the Royal Yacht Squadron, the premier yacht club in Great Britain. Cowes Week, held each year during August, is to yachting what Wimbledon Fortnight is to tennis. Racing takes place daily for yachts of all classes and designs. The first race was held on 10 August 1826, the prize being a gold cup to the value of £100.

jects. Like the van de Veldes, Wyllie created an enormous archive of annotated sketches and drawings from which he would work up finished pictures.

Wyllie was also fond of yacht racing. He co-owned a National 14ft dinghy, *Venture No. 127*, and raced for the Prince of Wales Cup when it was first contested in Cowes in 1927. Wyllie was a frequent visitor to the Isle of Wight, and in addition to painting the racing there, he also recorded in watercolours the launch of a number of yachts. He was present at the launch of Lipton's *Shamrock IV* in 1914 at Camper & Nicholson's yard in Gosport.

Wyllie was born into a family of gifted artists who provided him with his earliest artistic training. This was supplemented by formal tuition at Heatherly's Art School and the Royal Academy School in London. As well as being an expert with the brush, he was also a skilled printmaker and produced more than three hundred etchings and drypoints. His etchings of yachting scenes, especially of yachts racing, are the most valued of his prints.

Many of Wyllie's yachting oil paintings today hang in yacht clubs. The Royal Corinthian Yacht Club, now located in Cowes, for example, has a version of his oil painting *Butterflies and Working Bees* (*see page 126*), which depicts two big-class yachts, the royal vessel *Britannia* and the Earl of Dunraven's *Valkyrie II*, racing on the River Thames in around 1893. Both yachts were designed by G L Watson. With their elegant and imposing spreads of sail these 'butterflies' create a stark contrast to the 'working bees': the river craft and steam vessels whose service forms part of the daily routine of river life. Wyllie's original painting was sold and the version now on display is in fact a direct copy by his younger brother, Charles William Wyllie (1859–1923), who was also a marine painter. Charles had a precocious talent and exhibited his first picture at the Royal Academy at the age of thirteen.

William Lionel Wyllie's eldest son, Lieutenant-Colonel Harold Wyllie (1880–1973), inherited his father's passion for the sea and something of his artistic skills, too. He was especially fond of painting historical marine subjects, especially naval actions. Harold was passionate about maritime archaeology, and he acted as an advisor on the re-rigging of the *Victory*, Admiral Horatio Nelson's famous flagship, now on display in Portsmouth.

Harold Wyllie also painted the yachts of the big class era, notably the J-class yachts (*see page 126*). Wyllie junior was also a printmaker and ship modeller. He exhibited at the Royal Academy and was a founder member of the British Society of Marine Artists, later to be called the Royal Society of Marine Artists. Like Harold Wyllie, the London-born artist Bernard Finnegan Gribble (1873–1962) excelled at depictions of yachts, but preferred to paint historical subjects. These included dramatic naval actions of the Napoleonic era. Twenty of his works were exhibited at the Royal Academy between 1891 and 1904.

Lieutenant-Commander Rowland Langmaid (1897–1956) was one of William Lionel Wyllie's pupils, and he painted and etched in a similar style to his master. A C B Cull (1880–1931), who painted naval and yachting scenes, was an acolyte of Wyllie's, though not his pupil. Wyllie's contemporary, Arthur John Trevor Briscoe (1873–1943), surpassed him as a printmaker. He produced a large body of work, mostly of deck scenes of ships with sailors at work, and some yachting scenes. Briscoe was an enthusiastic yachtsman. His yacht *Golden Vanity* was built along the lines of a Brixham trawler. He wrote a *Handbook on Sailing* under the pseudonym 'Clove Hitch' and was a frequent contributor to *Yachting Monthly*. Briscoe taught a number of young painters, including the London-based artist Frederick Harnack (1897–1983), who sometimes signed his work using his nickname 'Fid'. He owned a gaff-rigged sloop, and produced illustrations for yachting magazines.

One yacht that drew considerable attention from contemporary artists, among them William Lionel Wyllie (*see page 126*), was Kaiser Wilhelm II's second racing yacht, the huge cutter *Meteor II*. Also designed by G L Watson, and built on the Clyde in 1896, she was larger than her rivals in every respect. In 1897, she raced the British royal yacht *Britannia* three times and lost only once. In the same year, as part of the institution of Kiel Week as a rival attraction to Cowes Week, the kaiser presented a trophy for a race from Dover, England, to the German port. Kaiser Wilhelm II was a

great lover of yachting and he did much to organise and promote offshore racing at the turn of the century. In 1891, he became Commodore of the German Imperial Yacht Club. There were several leading German artists who painted the kaiser's yachts. They included the Berlin painter Carl Salzmann (1847–1923), Hans Bohrdt (1857–c.1920) and the Hamburg artist Carl Schnars-Alquist (1855–c.1936) (*see page 127*). Schnars-Alquist left a career in banking to become an artist. He studied in Britain, Scandinavia and America and at the 'Master School' of Hans Gude in Berlin. An inveterate traveller, he was preoccupied mainly with marine subjects.

One of the most striking images of yachts of the big-class era of the 1920s was painted by Charles Pears (1873–1958) in monochrome, or grisaille, almost certainly for the *Illustrated London News* (*see page 127*). The work features the racing yachts *Britannia*, *Terpsichore* and *Nyria*. Principally known today for his poster designs for the London Underground and various rail and shipping companies, Pears was born in Pontefract, Yorkshire. In the First World War, he served with the Royal Marines as an official war artist and he worked for the War Artists Advisory Commission during the Second World War. An accomplished yachtsman, he wrote and illustrated several books on the subject, including *From the Thames to the Netherlands*, which contains illustrations of his oil paintings, monochromes and caricatures of people he met on the way. In 1938, John Player & Sons published a series of twenty-five cigarette cards after Pears' original yachting oil paintings. The artist's work is familiar for its clear design, uncluttered compositions and bold, vigorous and colourful brushwork, which suggest a sense of movement and excitement (*see page 128*).

In 1939, Pears became the first President of the Society of Marine Artists. The society was the result of the efforts of a number of painters, including William Lionel Wyllie, Harold Wyllie, Arthur Briscoe, and Pears, who sought to establish an organisation to promote the interests of marine artists. Although founded before the Second World War it did not hold its inaugural exhibition until 1946. It received its royal prefix in 1966. The society is still active today and its original aims remain unchanged: 'to encourage, develop and maintain the highest standards of marine art'. Since the mid-1980s, it has held its annual exhibition of members' work at the Mall Galleries in London.

Pears' American contemporary Frank Cresson Schell (1857–1942) also excelled as an artist and illustrator, notably producing illustrations for *Harper's Weekly*. Schell was a pupil of both the celebrated American painter Thomas Eakins (1844–1916) and Thomas Anschutz (1851–1912). A series of Schell's monochromes depicting various yachting subjects hangs in the New York Yacht Club, a gift from Bob Gregory, one of the club's members.

Norman Wilkinson (1878–1971) excelled as a yachting painter, printmaker and designer. He served in both world wars, in the first as an official war artist. He was present at the Gallipoli engagements during the landing at Sulva Bay on 7 August 1915. During the First World War, Wilkinson invented 'dazzle-camouflage' to help protect merchant and naval shipping from German U-boats. Bold designs were painted onto the sides of ships in order to break up the lines of the vessel and confuse enemy torpedo-men. In addition to naval and yachting subjects, he also painted landscapes and fishing scenes. He enjoyed to sail himself, and owned the *Wild Rose*, a 12-ton Falmouth Quay Punt, which was lost at the end of the war. Wilkinson wrote his autobiography, *A Brush with Life*, at the grand age of ninety-one.

In his capacity as honorary marine painter to the Royal Yacht Squadron, Wilkinson made many images of the *Britannia* racing, as well as of the royal steamship of the same name. The royal yacht competed in almost six hundred races between 1893 and 1935, and was one of the most successful racing yachts ever built. One of Wilkinson's dramatic portraits of her belongs to the British royal collection, but is currently on loan to the Royal Yacht Squadron (*see page 128*). The painting was presented to King George V during Cowes Week of 1923. Another splendid example of Wilkinson's skills as a yachting artist can be seen at the National Maritime Museum. This time the artist has depicted *Britannia* racing *Westward* in the Solent in 1935. *Britannia* is shown in her final Bermudian rig at close quarters alongside the elegant American schooner *Westward*, owned by F T B Davis. It was to be the royal yacht's last season. After the death of the king in January 1936, and in deference to his wishes, the forty-three-year-old yacht was towed out into the English Channel and scuttled. The *Britannia* was one of the most popular yachts of her era, however, and is still a favourite subject with painters today.

During the *Britannia*'s heyday, the royal steam yacht *Victoria and Albert III* was still in active service and she would invariably be present during the races at Cowes and other prominent regattas. One of the most remarkable images of the steam yacht was painted by the Australian artist Arthur James Weatherall Burgess in '*Britannia's Glory*' *The Royal Yacht* Victoria and Albert III *at Cowes, 1905* (*see pages 120–1*). Originally from New South Wales, Burgess emigrated to England in 1900. After studying in St Ives in Cornwall, he moved to London where he exhibited at the Royal Academy for the first time in 1905. Burgess was the art editor of *Brassey's Naval and Shipping Annual* between 1922 and 1930, and was an official war artist during the Second World War. He later painted a wide range of marine and landscape subjects, including skiing scenes. His use of vivid colours and broken brushwork indicate the influence of the Impressionists.

Montague Dawson (1895–1973) is arguably the most popular marine painter of the twentieth century. He is particularly remembered for his portraits of clipper ships battling against the elements on the high seas, and during his own lifetime he was afforded the unofficial title 'king of the clipper-ship school'. But Dawson's yachting subjects, many of which he produced early in his career, are less well known. These works have been profoundly influential on modern yachting art, and the British painter Roy Cross, along with many artists today, openly acknowledges a debt to Dawson. Contented patrons included prominent political figures, stars of stage and screen, and the British royal family. Critics have been less complimentary, however, dismissing Dawson's work as repetitive and claiming that he painted to a set formula. This is an accusation that can be levelled at all commercially successful artists, however; Dawson's detractors have clearly overlooked the less familiar areas of the artist's work, especially his depictions of the thrills and spills of ocean racing, regattas and yacht portraits.

Dawson was born in Chiswick, London, into an artistic family. His father, Henry Thomas Dawson, painted marine subjects, was a keen yachtsman and dabbled as an inventive engineer. The family home, known as Smuggler's House, was situated on Southampton Water and here Dawson spent his youth messing about in the family cutter. In around 1910, he joined a commercial art studio in London to work on posters and illustrations: this was an experience that was to prove useful to him during the

First World War. While Dawson was serving in the British Royal Navy as a junior officer, he drew and painted for the illustrated weekly newspapers and became a regular contributor to *The Sphere*.

During these formative years, Dawson came into contact with Charles Napier Hemy (1841–1917), an established marine painter then using a boat as a floating studio in Falmouth so that he could study ships, especially fishing vessels and yachts, at close quarters (*see pages 132–3*). Hemy was honorary marine painter to the Royal Yacht Squadron between 1913 and 1917, and exhibited at the Royal Academy. Dawson was deeply impressed by Hemy's work and claimed that it had 'opened a doorway for him'.

During the Second World War, Dawson was employed by the War Artists Advisory Commission to recreate naval battles. He became a professional artist and quickly established himself as a leading marine painter of his day. He exhibited at the Royal Academy and the Royal Society of Marine Artists. Leading yachtsmen were eager to commission Dawson to commemorate their ocean triumphs. The Vanderbilts in America and the British yachtsman T O M Sopwith, for example, were two of the artist's earliest patrons. The subject matter of many of his paintings reveals the influential yacht owners who came to him: the *Evaine*, owned by Owen Aisher, and the *Sceptre*, from the Royal Yacht Squadron, were depicted in a windswept Solent engaged in a trial run prior to crossing the Atlantic for the America's Cup; the Flying Fifteen *Cowslip* – designed by Uffa Fox, the celebrated naval architect and author – with Prince Philip at the helm, was painted sailing past the *Britannia* in a choppy sea. Dawson clearly enjoyed the challenge of depicting the excitement and speed of large competitive craft being pushed to the limit. But he also painted smaller vessels racing too, including the dragon-class yachts which were designed in 1929 by the Norwegian designer Johan Anker (*see page 131*). A number of countries produced similar small-class yachts around this time. They were introduced partly to cater for the less wealthy yachtsman who could not afford the big-class vessels. The American-born artist Frank Wagner, who later settled in England, painted small-class yachts and also Hunter-class gaffers (*see page 135*).

Since the end of the Second World War yachting art has been centred predominantly on Britain and the United States, reflecting the popularity of the sport in these two countries. The competitive legacy of the America's Cup lingers on, and not just in the racing itself. Yachting artists, too, on either side of the Atlantic, now compete for the most lucrative commissions.

From an early age, Peter MacDonagh Wood (1914–1982) combined his love of yachting and his skills as an artist. He raced dinghies, owned a 3-ton cutter, *Falcon*, and produced numerous yachting pictures for maritime magazines and books. He received membership of the Royal Society of Marine Artists in 1955. He has occasionally focused on the more leisurely aspects of yachting. His calm quayside scenes and images of cruising yachts (*see page 134*), with their warm, sunny effects, are a comforting contrast to the many images showing the vigours of ocean racing. Although Wood's contemporary, the Norwich-born artist Edward Seago (1914–1974) is better known for his coastal scenes and landscapes painted, he also painted yachts. His broken brushwork and interest in colour and atmosphere, derived from the French Impressionist movement of the third quarter of the nineteenth century, were not conducive to careful descriptions of nautical detail. Nonetheless, Seago, himself a yachtsman, was immensely popular with sailors. The artist's early life was spent travelling with circuses and in 1933 he wrote and illustrated a book about his experiences called *Sons of Sawdust*. He also illustrated poetry for John Masefield, served in the Royal Engineers during the Second World War and then turned to painting full time. Seago was invited on board the *Britannia* on a number of occasions. He remains a popular artist with the current British royal family and a selection of his paintings are on display on board the royal steam yacht. The royal steam vessel has been one of the most popular subjects for yachting portraitists since the war. Among the many artists to have painted her are the Dutch painter Jan Catharinus Adriaan Goedhart (1893–1975) (*see page 129*) and the popular and highly successful British marine artist John Stobart, who now lives and works in the United States (*see page 130*).

Several French marine painters with an interest in yachting are worthy of mention. Marin-Marie (1901–1987) (*see page 131*), Roger Chapelet (b.1903) and Jean Rigaud (b.1912) are the elder statesmen of an informal group who have inspired the younger generation of marine artists, among them Marc P G Berthier (b.1944) who paints and draws a wide variety of yachting scenes. Berthier has also illustrated books on yachting and in 1991 he was made an official maritime painter by the Département de la Marine.

'BUTTERFLIES AND WORKING BEES'

Charles William Wyllie (1859–1923) after William Lionel Wyllie (1851–1931)
(oil on canvas, 84.5 x 139cm, circa *1893)*
Royal Corinthian Yacht Club.

In this composition, the Wyllies have successfully contrasted the majestic power and elegance of the great yachts with the everyday life of working boats. *Britannia* and *Valkyrie II* met twenty-four times and each came in ahead on twelve occasions. The size of these yachts was breathtaking. *Britannia* was 121ft 5in overall. She carried 10,000sq ft of sail. Her boom was 92ft in length.

Charles William Wyllie painted in a style similar to his more famous brother, William Lionel Wyllie, although he preferred coastal and harbour subjects. Like Wilkinson, he assisted in the production of 'dazzle-camouflage' designs for ships during the First World War.

HMY *BRITANNIA* ESCORTED BY A DUTCH SQUADRON, 28 MARCH 1958

Jan Catharinus Adriaan Goedhart (1893–1975)
(oil on canvas, 51 x 101.5cm, dated 1958)
On loan to the National Maritime Museum, Greenwich.

Queen Elizabeth II is on her way to a state visit to the Netherlands. *Britannia* is shown here being escorted by the Dutch cruiser *De Ruyter* and destroyers.

This work was produced by Jan Catharinus Adriaan Goedhart, who was considered by many to be the leading light among Dutch marine artists of the 1950s. He worked mainly in The Hague and in the busy harbour at Rotterdam. In 1958, he was commissioned by the Netherlands Association of Sea Painters to commemorate this British state occasion.

THE BIG FIVE RACING IN THE SOLENT: *SHAMROCK V*, *BRITANNIA*, *ASTRA*, *VELSHEDA* AND *WESTWARD*

Lt-Col Harold Wyllie (1880–1973)
(oil on canvas, 46 x 81cm, circa *1930s)*
N R Omell Gallery.

Sir Thomas Lipton's J-class *Shamrock V* was built in 1930 by Camper & Nicholson specifically to challenge for the America's Cup. But she was no match for Harold S Vanderbilt's *Enterprise*, one of four American J-class yachts built that year to defend the cup.

Harold Wyllie shared his father's love of yachting, and was honorary marine painter to the Royal Yacht Squadron from 1934 to 1946.

METEOR IV WINNING THE A1-CLASS RACE AT THE 1912 INTERNATIONAL REGATTA AT KIEL

Carl Wilhelm Hugo Schnars-Alquist (1855–c.1936)
(oil on canvas, 51 x 76cm, dated 1912)
N R Omell Gallery.

Meteor IV, a steel schooner designed by Max Oertz, was built at the Germania Werft yard, Kiel, in 1909. She replaced her namesake designed by the American marine painter Archibald Cary Smith.

The German emperor wanted Kiel to rival Cowes Week, although Kiel was reported to have been 'too militaristic, having none of the charm, gaiety and informality of Cowes'.

THE YACHTS BRITANNIA, TERPSICHORE AND NYRIA OFF COWES, 1923

Charles Pears (1873–1958)
(monochrome on canvas, 28 x 62cm, circa 1923)
National Maritime Museum, Greenwich.

Painted in monochrome, this highly detailed work depicts yachts of the big-class era and was probably intended for the *Illustrated London News*. *Britannia*, to the far left, was owned initially by Edward VII and was re-rigged five times during her lifetime. George V raced her many times, even modifying her to the American Universal Rule to enable him to race against the J-class America's Cup contenders.

The painting would almost certainly have been accompanied by a key to help explain the race in progress. The technical detail in this picture is remarkable. Note the standing rigging of Mrs R E Workman's *Nyria* (previously identified as the *Ilyrica*), the Bermudian cutter in the foreground. She was fitted out with the new rig designed by C E Nicholson for the 1920 season.

THAMES BARGES COMING OUT OF HOLEHAVEN

Charles Pears
(oil on canvas, 114 x 145cm, circa *1940)*
Royal Society of Marine Artists Diploma Collection.

Pears had a remarkable facility for creating visually striking compositions. He combines his skill as a graphic designer with his knowledge of nautical detail: a rare combination indeed. Even today, the artist's pictures are surprising in their stylish design; they resonate with carefully arranged rhythmic patterns and lines, clearly influenced by the Art Deco style of the 1930s.

THE *BRITANNIA* PASSING THE EAST LEPE BUOY, SOLENT, 1921

Norman Wilkinson (1878–1971)
(oil on canvas, 150 x 203.5cm, dated 1921)
The Royal Collection.
Reproduced by Gracious Permission of
Her Majesty Queen Elizabeth II.

Wilkinson shows the *Britannia* racing at Cowes in 1921, one of the years in which she won. Between 1893 and 1924 the *Britannia* entered 337 races. She notched up 163 first prizes and 52 other prizes. Here she has just gybed round the East Lepe Buoy in a heavy squall. When Wilkinson presented the version of this painting to King George V, the king ordered him to re-position the buoy as he did not find the picture a faithful rendering of the event.

KAISER WILHELM II'S YACHT
METEOR II

William Lionel Wyllie
(pencil and watercolour, 23 x 32.5cm, circa 1896)
National Maritime Museum, Greenwich.

Meteor II, designed by G L Watson, replaced the German kaiser's first racing yacht of that name in 1896. She was larger and faster than leading yachts of her day, including both the *Britannia* and *Ailsa*. The kaiser owned four yachts named *Meteor*. The first, which the kaiser bought in 1892, was originally the *Thistle*, the 1887 America's Cup challenger, designed by G L Watson.

Wyllie produced many sketches and watercolours of the kaiser's yachts. He almost certainly went on board the vessels to make annotated studies. In one example, he includes a portrait of the kaiser aboard *Meteor II*.

Wyllie also sketched and painted British yachts both under sail and powered by steam. Many of his sketches are now in the National Maritime Museum. Wyllie was an eye-witness recorder during the movement of Queen Victoria's body from Osborne House, on the Isle of Wight, to Portsmouth aboard the royal steam yacht *Alberta*. His oil painting of the occasion, *The Passing of a Great Queen, 1901*, is now in the Walker Art Gallery, Liverpool.

A NICE BREEZE

Montague Dawson (1895–1973)
(watercolour with bodycolour, 43 x 66cm, circa 1920)
Reproduced by permission of the executors of the estate of Montague Dawson.
Photograph courtesy of Frost & Reed Ltd.

In this delicate watercolour, a racing dinghy is preparing to round the buoy. The yacht's gear, rigging and sails are rendered with meticulous detail.

Both the influence of Charles Napier Hemy and Dawson's training as an illustrator are evident in this carefully crafted portrayal of a day boat. Dawson largely gave up watercolour painting after around 1920.

HMY *BRITANNIA* AT THE OPENING OF THE ST LAWRENCE SEAWAY, 1959

John Stobart (b.1929)
(oil on canvas, 76 x 101.5cm, dated 1960)
National Maritime Museum, Greenwich.
Reproduced courtesy of the artist.

The current *Britannia* is the world's largest state and royal yacht and has been painted more times than any other maritime subject. Built in 1953 by John Brown on Clydebank to Admiralty specifications, she has a length of 412ft and a beam of 55ft. The yacht is powered by steam turbines and, for comfort at sea, is fitted with stabilisers. Decommissioned in 1997, the ultimate fate of *Britannia* is in doubt. It is known, however, that members of the royal family today are just as passionate about yachting as their forebears. Since 1953, Her Majesty Queen Elizabeth II has been Patron of the Royal Yacht Squadron, and the Duke of Edinburgh has been Admiral. Many of the royal family enjoy cruising.

John Stobart has depicted *Britannia* during her ceremonial opening of the St Lawrence Seaway in 1959. The artist's forceful composition enhances the excite-

ment of this notable occasion. The St Lawrence Seaway allows shipping to sail from Lake Ontario and the Great Lakes to the Gulf of St Lawrence and the Atlantic. The construction of the seaway was a collaborative project between Canada and the United States and at 300 kilometres in length it cost $470 million to build.

Stobart has a faithful and extensive following, and he is arguably the most successful living marine artist. Born in Leicester, England, he studied at the Derby College of Art and at the Royal Academy. During a voyage to Southern Rhodesia in 1950, Stobart realised the possibilities of producing paintings and prints of a range of vessels for shipping companies. He later moved to Canada and then to the United States where, encouraged by Margaret Wunderlich of the Kennedy Galleries, he recreated American harbour scenes in the days of the clipper ships.

AUGUST DAYS: DRAGON-CLASS YACHTS

Montague Dawson
(oil on canvas, 61 x 91.5cm, circa 1947)
Reproduced by permission of the executors of the
estate of Montague Dawson.
Photograph courtesy of Frost & Reed Ltd.

Few people could afford the big-class yachts. As yachting became more popular, the trend was for smaller classes of yachts with modest cabins. The *Dragon* was such a boat, designed by the Norwegian Johan Anker in 1929. It was an Olympic class until 1972. One of the most famous dragon-class yachts was Her Majesty Queen Elizabeth II and the Duke of Edinburgh's *Bluebottle*, which won a bronze medal for Britain in the Melbourne Olympics in 1956.

Dawson has created a tightly controlled composition. He has cleverly arranged the sunlight to highlight the leading yacht. The resulting reflections in the inviting blue and green sea lead directly back towards the viewer.

L'*ANAHITA*

Marin-Marie (1901–1987)
(gouache, 68 x 103.5cm, dated 1943)
ADAGP/Cliché Musée de la Marine, Paris.

L'Anahita, captained by Louis Bernicot, completed a circumnavigation between August 1936 and May 1938. She is shown here entering the Magellan Straits.

Marin-Marie was the name the artist legally adopted in 1940: such was his passion for maritime life. He was a keen single-handed yachtsman and based many of his pictures on first-hand experience. He exhibited widely in Europe and was a member of many yacht clubs, including the Royal Ocean Racing Club, and was Commodore of the St Malo Yacht Club. He is now one of the best known of all French marine painters. Marin-Marie's work is represented in many private and corporate collections.

LIFE

Charles Napier Hemy (1841–1917)
(watercolour and gouache, 71 x 102cm, circa 1913)
Royal Exchange Art Gallery.

This preparatory sketch for an oil painting shows the artist's interest in portraying in detail the boat's crew at work, as well as his fascination with the mood of the sea itself. The boat is a one-rater typical of the late Victorian period. Hemy's finished oil painting was exhibited at the Royal Academy in 1913.

Charles Napier Hemy was born in Newcastle-upon-Tyne. In 1852, his family emigrated to Australia. Hemy returned to England as a teenager and signed on board a brig. After studying at Newcastle School of Art under William Bell Scott, and later in Antwerp, he settled in Falmouth, where he lived aboard a floating studio.

Hemy's younger brother Thomas Marie Madawaska (1852–1937) also painted marines. A large-scale deck view of the *Britannia* with Edward VII aboard has recently come to light. It now hangs in the Langford Marine Gallery.

YACHTS ANCHORED OFF CEI NEWYDD IN WALES

Peter MacDonagh Wood (1914–1982)
(oil on canvas, 59.5 x 68.5cm, circa *1960)*
National Maritime Museum, Greenwich.

In this calm quayside picture, various dinghies and yachts are shown at anchor. Their masts create an interesting vertical distraction to the horizontal landscape beyond. Wood also brings the picture to life by including quayside strollers and people paddling in the sea.

Yachting and cruising are two of the fastest growing recreational and holiday activities. The romance associated with sailing at sea or in inshore waters has never been greater than today. For many people, a sailing holiday is an adventure of a lifetime.

A TRADITIONAL HUNTER-CLASS GAFFER ON THE NORFOLK BROADS, ENGLAND

Frank Wagner (1931–1996)
(gouache on panel, 46 x 66cm, circa 1996)
Royal Exchange Art Gallery.

Wagner was a keen sailor and part owner of *American Eagle*, a yacht that had previously taken part in the America's Cup trials in 1964. Sailing on inshore waters, as seen here on the waters of the Norfolk Broads, has grown considerably in popularity in the second half of the twentieth century. It is an inexpensive way for everyone to enjoy yachting.

CHAPTER IX

Yachting Nostalgia

IN THE LATE TWENTIETH CENTURY, THERE HAS BEEN A GENERAL DECLINE IN THE OVERALL NUMBER OF YACHTING PAINTINGS BEING PRODUCED, AS YACHT OWNERS AND RACE ORGANISERS NOW PREFER TO USE PHOTOGRAPHY, FILM AND VIDEO TO RECORD THE ACTION OF RACING. MOST YACHTING ARTISTS THEREFORE FIND THAT THEY MUST PAINT A WIDE RANGE OF OTHER SUBJECTS IN ORDER TO MAKE A LIVING, WHILE SOME ALSO WORK AS ILLUSTRATORS TO SUPPLEMENT THEIR INCOME.

That said, on the whole collectors and enthusiasts have become more interested in both the history and the art of yachting, and many are prepared to pay handsomely for the finest works of the few artists who specialise in the genre. Some yacht paintings can fetch tens of thousands of pounds at auction, and private commissions can often be double this sum.

Above all, most collectors want historic recreations of yachts, races and regattas of earlier times, painted in the traditional manner and full of nautical detail. Images of vessels under sail invariably command higher prices than those showing boats powered by steam. Yachting evokes a sense of romance and nostalgia that makes it a popular subject with collectors, even if they have little knowledge of the sport itself. The rolling sea and the beautiful arrangements of the sails seem to have a universal appeal. These craft appear to be from a 'Golden Age', a peaceful and harmonious world.

By far the most popular subjects for yacht painting today are the great races of the past, especially the America's Cup and the transatlantic races, and the celebrated yachts which took part, such as the schooners *America* and *Atlantic.* To these should be added the short-lived J-class yachts, the British royal racing yacht *Britannia* and the royal steam yacht of the same name. Perhaps it is not surprising then to discover that Britain and North America are still the major centres for the production of yachting art.

Previous pages
◆
Stars and Stripes
and Nippon
(*Detail*)
Michael Vaughan (b. 1940)
(*mixed media, 61 x 81.5cm, dated 1994*)
Courtesy of the artist.

The yachts depicted here are taking part in the America's Cup challenger trials. *Stars and Stripes*, captained by Dennis Conner, retrieved the cup from the Australians in 1987 after beating the New Zealand contender *Black Magic* in the trials. *Stars and Stripes* beat off the *New Zealand*, the Kiwi challenger of the following year.

It seems that *Nippon* is on the point of ramming *Stars and Stripes*. Vaughan's painting illustrates 'luffing', a manoeuvre where one yacht (in this case the yacht on the left) steers towards the wind to prevent the other yacht from passing. It is one of the most exciting and contentious moments of a race. The yachts almost appear to collide, providing a thrilling situation.

The British may have never won the America's Cup, but their artists have achieved acclaim for their outstanding contribution to yachting art, in both watercolours and oils. Many of today's British yachting painters are members of the Royal Society of Marine Artists (RSMA). David Cobb, for example, (b.1921) was president of the society between 1979 and 1983. After attending naval school, he studied engineering at Cambridge University. During the Second World War, he served in the Royal Navy, where he was in command of motor torpedo boats. His acquaintance with Charles Dixon inspired him to teach himself to paint, and in 1946 he decided to become a professional artist. At this time, he lived on a yacht at Newlyn, Cornwall. He later bought Arthur Briscoe's yacht *Golden Vanity*. As well as painting yachting scenes, Cobb also produces pictures of sailing ships and steamers, power boats and historical subjects. He worked in the Falkland Islands after the Argentine surrender in 1982 as an unofficial war artist, recreating the actions and the wartorn landscape. For a self-taught artist, Cobb has progressed a long way. He is the current honorary marine painter to the Royal Yacht Squadron, whose members have commissioned several works from him (*see page 142*).

Cobb's late contemporaries Leslie Wilcox (1904–1982) and John Chancellor (1925-1984) both excelled at painting historic yachts, including the famous yachts of the sixteenth and seventeenth centuries. Wilcox also painted a private commission of the royal steam yacht *Britannia* which currently hangs aboard the vessel. Robert Taylor (b.1945) and Robert Scott (b.1958), too, have both painted notable images of the *Britannia*, and these are very popular with collectors. Taylor studied at the Bath School of Art, and has exhibited at the RSMA, while Scott has sold his pictures through a number of London auction houses.

Roy Cross (b.1924) has for many years painted Anglo-American yacht races of the past, in a style inpired by Montague Dawson. Brought up in the London borough of Southwark, Cross was inspired to become a marine painter by his childhood experience of observing the ships and river craft on the Thames, then the busiest waterway in the world. He worked as a clerk in the offices of a shipping line and spent his free time developing his drawing and painting skills. During the Second World War, he was a technical illustrator in an aircraft factory. After the war, he studied at the Camberwell School of Arts and Crafts and St Martin's School of Art, both in London. He also continued to work as a freelance technical illustrator.

Cross's big break came when he was appointed chief illustrator for Airfix Products, the leading British manufacturer of model ship and aircraft kits. This work provided him with a degree of financial independence, allowing him to devote more time to marine painting. In 1976, he became a member of the RSMA. He is probably better known in America, where he has made a speciality of recreating historic scenes, such as old ports and harbours, clippers and packets, whaling expeditions, early steamships, and famous yacht races, especially the America's Cup (*see page 143*).

Another English yachting artist to be inspired by the work of Montague Dawson is Deryck Foster (b.1924). Foster studied painting in Bournemouth and, after the Second World War, at the Central School of Art in London. An accomplished yachtsman, he now lives in Bermuda, where he paints historic yachting scenes. Dawson's influence is particularly discernible in Foster's treatment of seas and skies, although the latter's handling of paint is less rigidly controlled.

The London-born artist David Brackman (b.1932) also recreates famous yacht races of the past, as well as producing portraits of modern vessels, such as the royal racing yacht *Britannia* (*see page 143*). He credits his fascination with the sea to the time he was evacuated to the east coast of England during the Second World War. He was originally drawn to ship modelling, for which he has won prizes, but later turned to painting. He has sailed widely in his own yacht, the *Panache*. John Michael Groves (b.1937) is one of several marine painters who also work as illustrators. Groves, a member of the RSMA, works in oil, pastel and pen-and-ink. Although mainly known for his historical subjects, he also paints yachts.

William Bishop (b.1942) is an all-round marine artist who excells at yacht portraits and races. Born near Portsmouth, he has had a lifelong love of boats and boating. His work has proved very popular with American collectors in particular, although his pictures are also in private and public collections all over the world. In 1988, Dennis Conner bought Bishop's painting of *Stars and Stripes* racing *Kookaburra II* off Perth.

The current President of the RSMA is the American artist Mark Myers (b.1945). Since 1971, Myers has lived in the southwest of England. Self-taught, he channels his practical deep-water sailing experience into his art works. He is well known as an illustrator of maritime books and magazines, and is also a member of the American Society of Marine Artists (ASMA), which was founded in 1978 with similar aims to the RSMA. The ASMA has no permanent home or exhibition venue. It regularly organises shows in collaboration with major American maritime museums, such as the Mystic Maritime Gallery in Connecticut. Myers specialises in images of round-the-world races (*see page 144*). He undertakes careful research on each subject he paints: he once corresponded at length with a yacht's skipper to ensure the accuracy of his picture, just as the van de Veldes had often done three hundred years earlier.

Geoff Hunt (b.1948) is known and admired for his lively book-cover illustrations to Patrick O'Brian's naval novels. He is also a successful marine artist and illustrator, and a member of the RSMA. After studying graphic design at art school, Hunt worked for some time in advertising and as an art editor and book designer. In 1979, he sold his house and, with his wife, cruised his yacht *Kipper* to the Mediterranean and back. After his return, he devoted himself to maritime art. His yachting subjects are meticulously constructed through extensive research. In addition to primary material, he also uses ship models to ensure nautical accuracy (*see page 145*).

J Steven Dews (b.1949) is widely hailed as the master of yachting art of today. Born in Yorkshire, Dews has family seafaring connections dating back to the seventeenth century. He takes inspiration for his work from his own yacht *Fine Art*, in which he also indulges his great passion for sailing. He is by far the most accomplished of a number of artists who paint in a style approaching photographic realism, and his art has often been imitated. Michael Whitehand (b.1941) and Stephen Renard (b.1947), among others, follow in his wake. Dews asserts that 'To paint marine scenes you have got to be a sailor. You have got to feel how the wind moves, how it affects the sea and how it affects the boat. You have also got to know the rules of the road! Otherwise, it is impossible to build a painting that is technically correct.... Every painting to me is an adventure –setting the mood of the sky and thus of the painting – but there are no short cuts, it is 5 per cent inspiration and 95 per cent hard work.' In addition to painting historical yachting scenes (*see page 145 and 146–7*), Dews also produces portraits of the big J-class yachts (*see page 148*) and more modern vessels. Such images are immensely popular with yachting enthusiasts, and Dews' work can be found in yacht clubs, maritime museums and corporate collections around the world. He also has a faithful circle of private collectors. Recently, his paintings have fetched well into five-figure sums at auction, while limited-edition prints of his work are also highly sought after.

Historical recreations, and other nostalgic yachting scenes (*see page 150*), are also the bedrock of the work of Tim Thompson (b.1951), a self-taught artist originally from Cottingham, Hull. His highly finished style is akin to earlier marine artists and his technique has been compared to the eighteenth-century English marine painter Nicholas Pocock. Thompson's works have illustrated a number of yachting books, including Ranulf Rayner's *The Paintings of The America's Cup, 1851–1987* and *The Story of Yachting*. The artist has also painted more up-to-date subjects which emphasise the poise and grace of modern racing yachts (*see page 151*).

Trevor Osborne (b.1952) has exhibited at the RSMA, although he is not currently a member. In 1985, he moved to the Isle of Wight, where he has crewed on J24s and several other boats. Working mainly in pastel and watercolour, Osborne combines his interest in light and colour with his enjoyment of being part of a crew. Like several yachting artists working today, he uses photographs as source material to assist him in his work. Many painters take their inspiration for subjects from historic photographs, especially those from archives such as Beken of Cowes. They may modernise, adapt or, in some instances, directly copy these images onto canvas.

Martyn Mackrill (b.1962) is a marine painter of great subtlety, sophistication and charm. Born on the Isle of Wight, he was destined to choose a profession linked to the sea: his father was a marine engineer in the

Merchant Navy, and his grandfather owned a fleet of trawlers. Mackrill showed an interest in drawing from an early age, and studied art at Portsmouth College and modelmaking at Sunderland Polytechnic. He has since returned to the Isle of Wight, where he produces carefully crafted historical works inspired by Charles Napier Hemy, Charles Dixon and William Lionel Wyllie (*see page 149*). He openly acknowledges their influence. He once said 'I am without doubt a traditionalist, and turn for guidance and inspiration to the painters of the last century. I also feel it is important to sail the same craft as my forefathers, enabling me to draw ships as a seaman: accurately, affectionately and with interest'.

Some painters have rejected such a traditionalist approach. One such artist is Michael Vaughan (b.1940), perhaps the most exciting yachting painter to have emerged in recent years. Inspired by the increasing sophistication of photography, film, video and computer graphics, Vaughan consciously works with these media to produce images of startling originality. Vivid, sometimes unreal colours, close-up shots, and unusual viewpoints all make Vaughan's work a far cry from the more traditional forms of yachting art. Rather than emphasising the gentle grace and serenity of yachts on water, his breathtaking compositions express the vigour, exhilaration and hard work of modern ocean-yacht racing (*see pages 136–7 and 154*). Often he concentrates solely on crew members as they go about their back-breaking duties (*see page 153*). To help him capture some of these views, he sometimes commissions photographers to take pictures of the vessels during races. Vaughan has become increasingly popular with collectors who appreciate the risks he has taken to produce works which break from the conventional modes of representing yachts.

Gerald Savine (b.1945) prefers to concentrate on a different aspect of modern racing. He once worked for various advertising companies and something of this experience is reflected in his art. His watercolours and gouaches show the dominance of advertising and corporate sponsorship in the sport of yachting. In Savine's tightly drawn images, the company logos and names seem to engulf the yachts themselves.

The world of advertising and commercial illustration has also had a significant influence on Rowena Wright (b.1970), one of the few women yachting artists. Herself a keen sailor, she is well placed on the Isle of

Wight to paint her favourite subjects. Wright's work often focuses on the personal experiences of a yacht's crew as they race through the water. Her portrait of the yachtswoman Tracy Edwards (*see page 152*) was exhibited at the RSMA's exhibition in 1996. That she has managed to reach such prominence in an almost exclusively male-dominated genre is testament to Wright's talent and determination. Traditionally, women were not allowed aboard naval ships, and most would have had little knowledge of merchant vessels. Because they were discouraged from going to sea in this way, it is not surprising that women felt marine painting was a male preserve. It would also have been difficult for them to have studied masts, rigging and how boats appeared on the high seas, all of which is essential training for a yachting artist.

Anthony D Blake (b.1951) is New Zealand's leading marine artist. He paints a wide range of maritime subjects, including clipper ships and port and harbour scenes, although he has made his reputation with yachts, both contemporary and historic. As a child, he sailed extensively off the coast of New Zealand. He even designed his own eighteen-foot catamaran. Presumably, Blake has benefited from commissions from his homeland, as New Zealand are the current holders of the America's Cup. He was chosen as the official artist for the 1993 Whitbread Round-the-World Race, an event he had painted on previous occasions (*see page 156*). At almost 32,000 miles, the Whitbread is the longest ocean race and has consistently attracted entries from all over the world. It is held every four years and will next be raced in 1997–8. Many celebrated international yachtsmen are associated with the race: among the best-known British names are Sir Robin Knox-Johnston, Chay Blyth, Clare Francis and Tracy Edwards.

Of the many American marine artists working today only time will tell which ones will be remembered. The self-taught artist and dealer William R Davis (b.1932) is certainly worthy of mention, however (*see page 155*). He draws upon the American marine painting tradition of the nineteenth century and acknowledges a debt to artists such as Fitz Hugh Lane, Martin Johnson Heade, Sanford R Gifford and John Frederick Kensett, not to mention James E Buttersworth and Antonio Jacobsen. In fact, his brushwork and colours are based on these artists. Davis has exhibited at the Mystic Maritime Gallery, which gave him his first one-man show.

Richard Loud's (b.1945) dramatic paintings of regattas and races have earned the artist widespread acclaim and various awards. Having served as a deckhand on a 114-foot motor yacht, Loud turned to designing and building yachts. Yet, all the time he was constantly drawing and painting the vessels around him. Donald Demers (b.1956) is also well known for his recreations of famous past races (*see page 149*). Chris Blossom (b.1956) is less familiar as a painter of yachts, although he is clearly capable of rivalling established artists with pictures such as *Silhouette* and *Port of Call* (*see page 148*). The latter is as much a landscape as a marine scene, portraying Roche Harbour with sailing boats from the gardens of the deHaro resort hotel. Jane Chapin (b.1954) is another of the few yachtswomen who paint yachting subjects. She is well known in American and 12-metre ocean racing. For a time, she studied under John Stobart. In 1985, she formed the International Society of Women Marine Artists. She is also a member of ASMA.

John Mecray (b.1937) shares Michael Vaughan's determination to break away from the traditional mode of representing yachts. He grew up in Cape May, New Jersey, close to the Atlantic Ocean. After studying at the Philadelphia College of Art, where he specialised in art and illustration, he then worked as a freelance illustrator, before devoting himself to full-time painting. He is an experienced yachtsman and was instrumental in founding the Museum of Yachting in Newport, Rhode Island. Mecray tries to portray what he believes to be 'some of the most magnificent objects ever created, classic sailing vessels, particularly the large racing yachts'. Close-up viewpoints and cropped compositions lend dynamism to his subjects, and are the hallmarks of his work. His cool, classical style is in part a result of his training as an illustrator. He is fascinated by the patterns and sculptural arrangements of masts, rigging and sails (*see page 158-9*). He is equally interested in conveying the sensation of yachts moving through the water (*see page 157*).

At the end of the twentieth century, the demand for recreations of historical yachting scenes still eclipses the many images of contemporary racing. With record prices continuing to be made at auction, this preference shows little sign of diminishing. However, there are many yachting subjects that have yet to be captured on canvas – survival at sea and daring rescues being just two examples. Perhaps it is now time to celebrate in oils the prevailing heroism of yachtsmen and women, and the vital role of the rescue services.

A Club Rally; Ocean Racers; Keelboats; A Seawanhaka Cup Race and the Naval Review, 1977

David Cobb (b.1921)
(oil on canvas, 49 x 59.5cm, dated 1977)
Royal Yacht Squadron.

In 1977, the Royal Yacht Squadron commissioned David Cobb to commemorate the commodoreship of Lord Cathcart, 1974–1980. The artist came up with an imaginative solution, painting this charming series of yachting vignettes.

AMERICA'S CUP 1901: *COLUMBIA* VERSUS *SHAMROCK II*

Roy Cross (b.1924)
(oil on canvas, 81.5 x 127.5cm, dated 1993)
Courtesy of the artist.

The America's Cup series of races in 1901 was very closely contested and this encouraged Sir Thomas Lipton to have a third attempt at winning the cup in 1903 with *Shamrock III*. Yet again, he was unsuccessful, however. Roy Cross has painted the schooner *America*, the Hundred-Guinea Cup race, and the subsequent America's Cup challengers on a number of occasions.

BRITANNIA UNDER PRESSURE

David Brackman (b.1932)
(gouache, 48.5 x 75cm, dated 1997)
Courtesy of the artist.

The British royal racing yacht remains a favourite subject with contemporary marine painters. Brackman is one of several artists whose popularity enables them to sell their work at auction. They invariably choose well-known subjects such as this, which appeal to the American market in particular.

Collectors are looking for carefully crafted yachting pictures, full of detail and convincing in terms of the unity of vessel, sea and sky. But, above all else, it is nostalgic subjects that sell well.

ROUND-THE-WORLD RACE: THE *GREAT BRITAIN II* AND *KRITER II* IN THE TASMAN SEA, 26 SEPTEMBER 1975

Mark Myers (b.1945)
(oil on canvas, 61 x 51cm, dated 1976)
National Maritime Museum, Greenwich.

The subject of this painting is a round-the-world yacht race which started out on 31 August 1975. Its purpose was to travel the distance between London and Sydney via the Cape of Good Hope in a shorter time than had been achieved by an old cargo-carrying clipper ship, which had covered the 13,650-mile stretch in sixty-nine days. The race was to start and finish in Sheerness, England, and there was to be only one stop, in Sydney. Not sur-prisingly, the race was to prove quite an ordeal for those who participated. This scene shows two of the four yachts that took part in the race. Along with *Great Britain II* and the French ketch *Kriter II*, were the Italian *CSeRBII Busnelli* and the Dutch *The Great Escape*. *Great Britain II* was first home on both legs, and her outward time of just over sixty-seven days narrowly beat the record of the clipper ship.

OUTWARD LEG

Geoff Hunt (b.1948)
(gouache on board, 39.5 x 44.5cm,
dated 1986)
Courtesy of the artist.

The *Outward Leg* was the extraordinary boat of the equally extraordinary Tristram Jones. With typically mordant humour, Jones named the boat after the leg he had lost in a road accident, causing him to switch boats from a monohull to a trimaran.

Hunt has painted many yachting subjects, including images of the royal steamship *Britannia*, as well as cruising yachts. He painted *Tzu Hang*, Miles Smeeton's celebrated cruising yacht, on one of her circumnavigations. The picture of *Tzu Hang* appeared as a book-cover illustration and is now in the private collection of the Smeeton family.

ATLANTIC OFF THE LIZARD, 1905

J Steven Dews (b.1949)
(oil on canvas, 76 x 127cm, dated 1996)
Tryon and Swann Gallery.
Courtesy of the artist.

Kaiser Wilhelm II, the German emperor, and owner of *Meteor II*, presented a gold cup in 1905 for a transatlantic race from Sandy Hook, just outside New York Harbour, to the Needles off the Isle of Wight. The race attracted eleven entries, including Lord Brassey's *Sunbeam*. The American-owned yacht *Atlantic*, shown here, was skippered by Charlie Barr and finished the course in twelve days, four hours and one minute, a record that would stand for more than seventy years.

BRENTON REEF CUP, *NAVAHO* AND *BRITANNIA* OFF THE NEEDLES, 1893

J Steven Dews (b.1949)
(oil on canvas, 101.5 x 152.5cm, dated 1996)
Private collection.

During July 1893, the American yacht *Navaho* arrived at Cowes to race the new *Britannia*. Although the two yachts were very closely matched, *Britannia* beat the American yacht twelve times out of the thirteen races they met. At noon on 14 September, both yachts started from the Needles on the 120-mile race to Cherbourg and back. The race was to be run using the American rules, the winner being calculated on an 'elapsed time' system, as opposed to 'first over the finishing line'.

A strong easterly gave both vessels a 'broad reach' there and back. *Britannia* was first away after the gun with *Navaho* almost a minute behind. After the sixty-mile dash to Cherbourg, *Navaho* was twenty-five seconds in front, but as they left the eastern end of the breakwater *Britannia* had clawed back a two-and-a-half minute lead. They finished the race in the dark with *Britannia* leading by fifty-seven seconds, but only two-and-a-half seconds on 'corrected' time. *Navaho* protested, however, as she claimed the 'finish mark' boat had moved, and that as a consequence she had sailed a longer course than *Britannia*. The Royal Yacht Squadron, after a lengthy meeting, agreed and awarded her the Brenton Reef Cup.

BIG CLASS: DOWNWIND START OFF THE SQUADRON

J Steven Dews (b.1949)
(oil on canvas, 91.5 x 70cm, dated 1996)
Private collection.

By 1935, after twenty-five years of competitive racing, the 323-ton schooner *Westward* had become no match for the new J-class yachts. The 42-year-old cutter *Britannia*, although 'J' rigged, also could not keep pace with the likes of the newer *Velsheda* and *Candida*. This was to be both *Britannia*'s and *Westward*'s last racing season. On 20 January 1936, King George V died and, to comply with his wishes, *Britannia* was scuttled just south of the Isle of Wight. As a mark of respect for the king, T B Davis, the owner of *Westward*, stopped racing the magnificent schooner. She spent the rest of her career cruising around Europe.

PORT OF CALL

Christopher Blossom (b.1956)
(oil on canvas, 51 x 101.5cm, dated 1995)
Courtesy of the artist.

Roche Harbour on the San Juan Island, Washington, at the border of America and Canada, is the 'port of call' of this work's title. 'I'm trying to convey a sailor's view of a contemporary sailing area' says Blossom, who acknowledges that his picture is as much a landscape as it is a seascape. His inventive approach to compositions brings a new visual excitement to most subjects.

Blossom's father and grandfather were successful commercial illustrators. As a teenager, he was taken to see a John Stobart exhibition in Manhattan, and he became captivated by the artist's work. He studied at the Charles Parsons School of Design in New York City. Initially, he followed his family's footsteps and worked as an illustrator producing book covers and magazine illustrations on maritime and aviation subjects. But he later became a full-time marine painter, working mainly in oils. He is best known for his historical port and harbour scenes, but he has also painted contemporary subjects, including fishing vessels and yachts. He sails himself, in the *Arcadia*, a 33ft sloop.

BEFORE THE START: *BRITANNIA* AND *VIGILANT*, HUNTER'S QUAY, RIVER CLYDE, 1894

Martyn Mackrill (b.1962)
(watercolour, 35.5 x 58.5cm, dated 1996)
Courtesy of the artist.

On 9 July 1894, the royal racing yacht *Britannia* defeated the Herreshoff-designed *Vigilant*, then owned by the Gould brothers of New York. *Vigilant* had been a successful defender of the America's Cup in 1893, defeating the Earl of Dunraven's *Valkyrie II*. George Watson designed both her and the *Britannia*. The *Glasgow Herald* reported: 'the victory of *Britannia* was once more hailed with cheers from the spectators, and with a loud and prolonged tooting of horns and steam yachts whistling'.

This is one of Mackrill's masterworks. Although he openly recognises many artistic influences, he has succeeded in producing pictures of great originality and charm that make a refreshing change from the current vogue for the photographic style of painting. In some of his works, there is a heightened stillness that is reminiscent of the nineteenth-century American painter Thomas Eakins (1844–1916), who produced a small number of remarkable sailing, yachting and rowing subjects.

REACHING FOR VICTORY: THE SCHOONER *MAGIC*, 1870, FIRST DEFENSE OF THE AMERICA'S CUP

Don Demers (b.1956)
(oil on canvas, 71 x 127cm, dated 1994)
Courtesy of the artist.

The first British attempt to recapture the America's Cup was undertaken by James Ashbury, with his yacht *Cambria*. She was designed by Michael Ratsey and belonged to the Royal Thames Yacht Club. *Magic* defeated *Cambria* and twenty-two other yachts.

Demers developed maritime experience as a crew member aboard many deep-water sailing vessels. He attributes his passion for art to his high-school art teacher, and to his training at the art school of the Worcester Art Museum, in Massachusetts. He started his artistic career as an illustrator and later worked for many popular maritime magazines such as *Reader's Digest*, *Sail Magazine*, *Yankee* and *Down East*. He is a fellow of the American Society of Marine Artists (ASMA), and has won a record nine awards at the Mystic International Marine Art Exhibition.

YACHTS OF THE ROYAL THAMES YACHT CLUB RACING OFF GREENWICH

Tim Thompson (b.1951)
(oil on canvas, 76 x 122cm, circa 1984)
Courtesy of the artist.

This is not so much a historical recreation but rather a nostalgic view of yachting on the Thames. The yachts are depicted off Greenwich Hospital, which was a home for old and disabled seamen until the third quarter of the nineteenth century. The domes designed by Sir Christopher Wren are clearly visible in the background, and are reminiscent of St Paul's Cathedral, Wren's most famous design.

Thompson has taken great topographical and architectural liberties in this scene, as Canaletto had done when painting his view of Greenwich Hospital in about 1750.

BRITANNIA AND *SHAMROCK IV* OFF THE ROYAL YACHT SQUADRON

Tim Thompson
(oil on canvas, 76 x 101.5cm, dated 1987)
Courtesy of Ashcombe Fine Arts.

In this work, Thompson has graphically illustrated one of the more unusual uses of British royal yachts. After King George V's death in 1936, Edward VIII made no attempt to challenge his father's wish that his grand royal racing yacht be scuttled; Edward was more interested in golf than in yachting. He can be seen here at the stern of the yacht, driving golf balls into the water. The giant sail of *Britannia* draws the viewer towards Edward just at the moment he is mid-swing. The Royal Yacht Squadron can be seen in the background.

AMERICA'S CUP 1995: NEW ZEALAND TRIUMPHS

Tim Thompson
(oil on canvas, 56 x 76.5cm, dated 1995)
Courtesy of the artist.

In 1995, the challenger from New Zealand, *Black Magic*, impressively defeated Dennis Conners' *Young America* to take the 'Auld Mug' (the Hundred-Guinea Cup) away from the Americans. The secret tactic that allowed them to achieve such a famous victory was, according to the Kiwis, 'simply teamwork'.

The masts and sails of these yachts are well portrayed in a dramatic image. It appears as if the yachts might collide, but the slight difference in mast heights indicates that *Black Magic* will pass clearly ahead. The advertising logos on the sails emphasise the importance of commercial sponsorship in today's high-profile races.

TRACY EDWARDS ON BOARD *MAIDEN*

Rowena Wright (b.1970)
(oil on canvas, 100 x 100cm, dated 1996)
Courtesy of the artist.

In 1989, the first all-woman crew sailed in the Whitbread Round-the-World Race in the boat *Maiden*, captained by Tracy Edwards. It took them just less than nine months to complete the course. Ocean racing demands enormous skill, endurance and a keen understanding of the weather. Everything is done to make the boat go as fast as possible, whether adjusting the sails, plotting the course or steering. The concentration on Edward's face is clear as she keeps her eyes steady ahead and her hands firmly on the wheel. In her own words, Rowena Wright has attempted to combine portraiture and sailing, her two favourite subjects, in this picture. She works as an artist and illustrator. Sadly, there are few women artists with such a passion for yachting scenes. Alice Fanner (1865–1930) is perhaps the best known. She painted in a style that at its best rivals the freshness and vigour of Norman Wilkinson. She studied at several art schools, including the Slade.

RETRIEVING A SPINNAKER

Michael Vaughan (b.1940)
(mixed media, 46 x 68.5cm, dated 1995)
Courtesy of the artist.

This is one of the many potentially dangerous activities on board a modern racing yacht. Vaughan's vigorous style heightens the sense of urgency of what is in fact a routine activity. The artist himself says: 'I'm not interested in painting pretty pictures; it is the working aspect of the yacht that is of special interest to me'. Those who have crewed on racing yachts can easily empathise with Vaughan's work as their exertions are his primary focus. Vaughan often employs a close-up technique, as he has done here, rather than adopting a more traditional, distant viewpoint, in an attempt to reveal the reality of life on a racing ocean-yacht. This method makes the viewer feel almost part of the crew, helping the others haul the spinnaker back on board.

ROUND THE HORN

Michael Vaughan
(mixed media, 51 x 66cm, dated 1995)
Courtesy of the artist.

Another of Vaughan's startling close-up views shows the deck of a racing yacht as it rounds the Horn. The crew stand huddled together at her stern, as a wave is about to break on deck. The scene is far from imaginary as the artist based his composition on several photographs taken from the bow of a yacht during a terrible storm at sea. Vaughan sees no reason to reveal the type and name of the yacht, as would have been necessary in a traditional yacht portrait. His interest lies in creating an atmosphere, not in recording the exact appearance of the vessel. However,

he sometimes focuses on specific details to such a degree that his works can have a super-real effect. Here he has brilliantly captured the gloomy, green-tinged light visible through the storm, the effect of rain and spray lashing against the yacht, and, it seems, even the sound of the howling wind as it swirls around the masts.

Vaughan's forceful graphic style and colourful palette have given his work a wide appeal. His market not only includes yachting enthusiasts, but also art collectors who have no specific interest in sailing.

A BEETLECAT RACING OFF HYANNISPORT, MASSACHUSETTS

William R Davis (b.1932)
(oil on canvas, 20.5 x 30.5cm, dated 1991)
Courtesy of the artist.

Beetlecats are small gaff-rigged boats sailed on the east coast of America. Davis learnt to sail in one very similar to this. He grew up in Hyannis Port, Massachusetts. The artist often paints on a small scale and has been inspired by many painters of the nineteenth century. He especially acknowledges Buttersworth as a major influence on his work. For the last six years, Davis has run an art gallery in Dennis, Massachusetts, specialising in nineteenth-century American European painting.

THE NEW YORK YACHT CLUB'S SESQUICENTENNIAL LAYDAY AT HARBOR COURT, 1994

Anthony D Blake (b.1951)
(oil on canvas, 51 x 101cm, dated 1994)
Courtesy of the Gregory Gallery, Connecticut, United States.

Blake has painted a late-afternoon scene with *Black Knight* and *Whitecap* alongside the dock at Harbor Court. Harbor Court was the former Newport home of Commodore John Nicholas Brown. In 1987, the house was sold to a group part- nership, which donated the building to the New York Yacht Club later that year. Flags of the six yacht clubs competing in the regatta are flying from the yardarm. A few light gusts create a streaky appearance on the water.

STEINLAGER II IN THE SOUTHERN OCEAN, 1989

Anthony D Blake
(oil on canvas, 56 x 76cm, dated 1990)
Courtesy of the artist and the Gregory Gallery, Connecticut, United States.

Steinlager II is portrayed surfing past an iceberg in the 'Roaring Forties' during the 1989–1990 Whitbread Round-the-World Race, highlighting the perils of ocean racing. Skippered by the artist's brother, the eminent yachtsman Peter Blake, the yacht completed an unprecedented victory by winning each of the six legs. The average speed for the whole race was a remarkable 10.7 knots.

Blake has the advantage of having been born into a family which combined a passion for sailing and the arts. After working as a civil engineer, he taught himself to paint. He was selected as the official Whitbread artist for the 1993 Whitbread Round-the-World Race. He lives in New Zealand and has had two one-man shows at the Gregory Gallery in Connecticut, United States.

A CLASS START, AUCKLAND ANNIVERSARY REGATTA, 29 JANUARY 1907

Anthony D Blake
(oil on canvas, 56 x 84cm, dated 1993)
Courtesy of the artist and the Gregory Gallery, Connecticut, United States.

This painting depicts the start of the 'A' class fleet for the Auckland Anniversary Regatta. The flagship, decked out in flags and packed with sightseers, is the Huddart Parker steamship *Victoria*. The yachts, from left to right, are *Moana*, *Thelma*, *Rainbow* (in the foreground), *Ariki* and *Aorere*. *Thelma* won the race. Also in the foreground is a small launch powered with the 'new' petrol engine. In the background, on the right, is the paddle-wheel ferry *Victoria*.

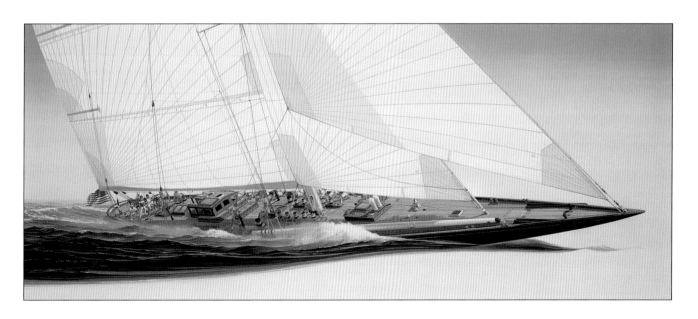

SHAMROCK V – 1995

John Mecray (b.1937)
(oil on canvas, 51 x 122cm, dated 1995)
Courtesy of the artist.

Sir Thomas Lipton's fifth and final challenge for the America's Cup in 1930 ended in failure, like his four previous attempts. Mecray's depiction has a futuristic quality. It is as if the yacht is almost moving into another spatial dimension. The artist has had a long association with the *Shamrock*. As a prime mover behind the establishment of the Museum of Yachting, he was involved with the transportation of the vessel to Newport, Rhode Island, and her subsequent restoration to J-class yacht standards. Mecray is also the founder and trustee of the yacht's current owners, the International Yacht Restoration School (IYRS).

NEW YORK HARBOUR

(Detail)

John Mecray (b.1937)
(oil on canvas, 51 x 94cm,
dated 1983)
Courtesy of the artist.

The intriguing viewpoint of this composition is from the deck of the ship *Citizen* as she enters New York Harbour on 14 May 1851. The newly launched schooner yacht *America*, still in primer, can be seen running out of the East River for her trials against the sloop *Maria*. The artist has gone to considerable pains to recreate the landmarks in the background – from the Hudson River on the left, to Castle Garden and Battery Park, and the US Custom House on the right.

Mecray has portrayed a nineteenth-century scene in a highly contemporary style. Although there are figures on board the *Citizen*, you have to look closely to see them. They are overshadowed by the scale and intricate depiction of the masts and rigging. Mecray has managed to draw the viewer into the scene, making him feel as if he is also standing on the deck of the ship.

Index of featured artists

Select bibliography

Archibald, E H H, *Dictionary of Sea Painters*, Antique Collectors' Club, Woodbridge, Suffolk, 1989
Brewington, Dorothy E R, *Dictionary of Marine Artists*, Peabody Museum of Salem, Mystic Seaport Museum, 1982
Brewington, Dorothy E R, *Marine Paintings and Drawings in the Mystic Seaport Museum*, Mystic Seaport Museum, 1986
Brook-Hart, Denys, *Nineteenth-Century British Marine Painting*, Antique Collectors' Club, 1992
Brook-Hart, Denys, *Twentieth-Century British Marine Painting*, Antique Collectors' Club, 1981
Cockett, F B, *Early Sea Painters 1660–1730*, Antique Collectors' Club, 1995
Cordingly, David, *Marine Painting in England, 1700–1900*, Studio Vista, London, 1974
Cordingly, David, *Painters of the Sea*, Lund Humphries, London, 1979
Dalton, A D F, *British Royal Yachts*, unpublished
Dear, Ian, *The Royal Yacht Squadron 1815–1985*, Stanley Paul & Co Ltd, 1985
Finch, Roger, *The Pierhead Painters: Naive Ship-Portrait Painters 1750–1950*, Barries & Jenkins, London, 1983
Gaunt, William, *Marine Painting*, Secker & Warburg, London, 1975
Gavin, C E, *Royal Yachts*, Rich & Steele, 1932
Grassby, Richard B, *Ship, Sea & Sky: The Marine Art of James Edward Buttersworth*, South Street Seaport Museum in association with Rizzoli, New York, 1994
Harrington, Melissa H, *The New York Yacht Club: 1844–1994*, Greenwich Publishing Group Inc, 1994
Harris, Daniel G and F H Chapman, *The First Naval Architect And His Work*, Conway Maritime Press, London, 1989
Heckstall-Smith, B, *Yachts & Yachting in Contemporary Art*, The Studio Ltd, 1925
Jacobsen, Anita, *Frederick Cozzens Marine Painter*, Alpine Fine Arts Collection, New York, 1982
Johnson, Peter, *Yachting World: The Encyclopedia of Yachting*, Dorling Kindersley, London, 1989
Johnson, Peter, *Twenty Years of the Ultimate Ocean Race: Whitbread Round the World 1973–1993*, Whitbread plc, 1992
Kemp, Peter and Ormond, Richard, *The Great Age of Sail*, Phaidon, Oxford, 1986
Keyes, George S, *Mirror of the Empire, Dutch Marine Art of the Seventeenth Century*, Cambridge University Press, 1990
Knox-Johnston, Robin, *History of Yachting*, Phaidon, Oxford, 1990

McCutchan, Philip, *Great Yachts*, Crown Publishers, Inc, New York, 1979
Peluso, Jr, A J, 'Thomas Willis: "A Correct Picture of Any Vessel Guaranteed"' Maine Antique Digest, November 1980
Peluso, Jr, A J, 'Don't Collect Currier & Ives or Endicott: Collect Charles Parsons', Maine Antique Digest, December 1987
Phillips-Birt, Douglas, *The Cumberland Fleet Two Hundred Years of Yachting 1775–1975*, The Royal Thames Yacht Club, London, 1978
Quarm, Roger and Wilcox, Scott, *Masters of the Sea: British Marine Watercolours*, Phaidon, Oxford, 1987
Robinson, M S, *Van de Velde Drawings: A Catalogue of the Drawings in the National Maritime Museum*, Cambridge University Press, 1974
Robinson, M S, *The Paintings of the Willem van de Veldes*, National Maritime Museum, Greenwich, 1990
Rousmanière, John, *The Luxury Yachts*, Time-Life Books, Amsterdam, 1981
Schaefer, Rudolph J, *J E Buttersworth: Nineteenth-Century Marine Painter*, Mystic Seaport Museum, 1975
Taylor, James, *Marine Painting: Images of Sail, Sea and Shore*, Studio Editions, 1995
Taylor, James, and McHugh, Patrick, *Yachts on Canvas: A Visual Celebration from the Seventeenth Century to the Present Day*.
    Companion guide to an exhibition curated by the National Maritime Museum at the London office of A T Kearney, spring 1997
Warner, Oliver, *An Introduction to British Marine Painting*, London, 1948
Waterhouse, Ellis, *British Eighteenth-Century Painters*, Antique Collectors' Club, 1991
Whipple, A B C, *The Racing Yachts*, Time-Life Books, Amsterdam, 1980
Wilkinson, Norman, *A Brush with Life*, Seeley Service & Co, London, 1969
Wilmerding, John, *Robert Salmon, Painter of Ship and Shore*, Peabody Museum of Salem, 1971
Wilmerding, John, *A History of American Marine Painting*, Harry N Abrams Inc, New York, 1987
Wilmerding, John, *Paintings of Fitz Hugh Lane*, Harry N Abrams, 1988
Wood, Christopher, *Dictionary of Victorian Painters*, Antique Collectors' Club, 1992
The Art of the Van de Veldes, exhibition catalogue, National Maritime Musuem, Greenwich, 1982
A Celebration of Marine Art: Fifty Years of the Royal Society of Marine Artists, Blandford, 1996
Concise Catalogue of Oil Paintings in the National Maritime Museum, compiled by the staff of the NMM, Antique Collectors' Club, 1988
The Dictionary of British Artists 1880–1940, Antique Collectors' Club, 1980